Summary

(Figures in parenthesis refer to the numbered paragraphs in the text of the Report)

1. Introduction

Premature deaths and disabling illnesses caused by cigarette smoking have now reached epidemic proportions and present the most challenging of all opportunities for preventive medicine in this country. The challenge has remained unanswered since the first report, *Smoking and Health,* by the Royal College of Physicians was published in 1962. The Government has done little to curb cigarette smoking, which continues to increase. The present report reviews the evidence of the effects of smoking on health and makes proposals for action in the hope that the public conscience will be aroused and that effective preventive action will be taken.

History of smoking (1. 4 to 1. 5). Since its introduction in the sixteenth century, smoking has always had its advocates and opponents; only recently has scientific study produced valid evidence of its effects upon health. Cigarettes have largely replaced other forms of smoking in the past seventy years; the level of consumption rose steeply over this period, has now levelled off in men, but is still rising in women (Figure 1. 1).

Smoking habits (1. 6 to 1. 10). After publication in 1962 of the Royal College Report, *Smoking and Health,* there was a sharp drop in the number of men smoking cigarettes but, though reduction is maintained in social classes I, II, and III, the numbers of cigarettes smoked by men overall is still close to the 1961 level. Fewer women than men smoke but their numbers are rising (Figure 1. 2). Filter-tipped cigarettes have become increasingly popular and more cigars are now smoked than formerly (Figure 1. 3). Smoking is continuing to increase among girls, but not boys, at school.

Since 1951 cigarette smoking by doctors has steadily declined and in 1965 only one-third smoked cigarettes compared with two-thirds of other men (Figures 1. 4 and 1. 5).

Tobacco advertising (1. 11, 1. 12). Despite prohibition of

31, 120

cigarette advertising on TV after July 1965, sales promotion for tobacco by advertising and by gift coupons with cigarettes has continued to increase (Table 1. 1 and Figure 1. 6), but a code of more ethical advertising has been adopted. In 1968, £52 million was spent by the tobacco industry on sales promotion.

Research into the effects of smoking has been supported by the Medical Research Council and the Tobacco Research Council but little research has been initiated into the prevention of diseases caused by smoking (1. 13, 1. 14).

Action by Government (1. 15 to 1. 20). This has been virtually confined to an annual outlay of up to £100,000 on health education about the dangers of smoking; this may be compared with £1,300,000 spent on education about road safety. The small number of anti-smoking clinics set up after 1962 have had little official support and most have been discontinued. Ministers, without reference to the fatal effects of cigarette smoking or to the economic loss it occasions, have stated that the large revenue from taxation provided by undiminished sales of cigarettes is indispensable.

2. Smoking, Illness, and Shortening of Life

Death rates in relation to smoking habits. The fatal effects of tobacco smoking are almost restricted to cigarette smokers, and increase with the amounts smoked. Cigarette smokers are about twice as likely to die in middle age as are non-smokers and may have a risk similar to that of non-smokers ten years older. It is estimated that over 20,000 deaths in men between the ages of 35 and 64 are caused every year by smoking in the United Kingdom. The chances are that two out of every five heavy cigarette smokers, but only one out of every five non-smokers, will die before the age of 65. The man of 35 who is an average cigarette smoker is likely on average to lose $5\frac{1}{2}$ years of life compared with a non-smoker (2. 2 to 2. 7, Figures 2. 1, 2. 2 and 2. 3).

Those who discontinue smoking cigarettes run a steadily diminishing risk of dying from its effects, even after many years of smoking, and attain the level of non-smokers after ten years of abstinence (2. 8). The effect of this is shown in the declining death rates from disease related to smoking among British doctors as compared with others. Doctors are now smoking much less than others (Table 2. 3). Most of the excess risk of the cigarette smoker is due to his smoking habits and not to other characteristics that might render him more susceptible to illness (2. 10). The diseases to which the smoker is most liable not only may be fatal but may also cause much sickness and disablement (2. 11). Cigarette smokers are therefore much less likely than non-smokers to enjoy retirement unspoilt by illness (2. 15).

3. The Chemistry and Pharmacology of Tobacco Smoke

Tobacco smoke has a complex composition. Its most important components are substances that can cause cancer in experimental animals, irritants that may cause bronchitis, nicotine that has many adverse effects on the heart and blood vessels and is probably responsible for tobacco habituation, and carbon monoxide that interferes with the blood's capacity to carry oxygen to the tissues of the body. Lung cancer has now been produced in animals which have inhaled tobacco smoke.

4. Smoking and Cancer of the Lung

The world-wide rise in the number of deaths from lung cancer has continued. Although in British men under the age of 65 the number is now declining slowly, it is still increasing at older ages and in women at all ages. Expert committees in many countries are all agreed that cigarette smoking is the cause of this modern epidemic (4. 1, 4. 2).

Many surveys have established a clear, quantitative relationship between numbers of cigarettes smoked and incidence of lung cancer (4. 3 to 4. 6).

The risk is raised by habits, such as inhaling, that increase the lungs' exposure to the smoke (4. 7 to 4. 9). It may be reduced but not removed by changing to filtered cigarettes (4. 10) and declines rapidly during the ten years after smoking is discontinued (4. 11, 4. 12) (Figure 4. 3).

Pipes and cigars appear to play only a small part in causing lung cancer, as does general pollution of the air. Several agents encountered in industry may bring on the disease but contribute little to its overall incidence (4. 13 to 4. 16).

Interpretation of the evidence. There is no doubt of the close association between exposure to cigarette smoke and lung cancer. Certain objections to the conclusion that cigarette smoking is a cause of lung cancer are examined and found to be without substance (4. 18 to 4. 28).

If present smoking habits continue, it has been forecast that there will be some 50,000 deaths from the disease each year in England and Wales in the 1980s. If cigarette smoking were to cease there might in twenty years time be no more than 5,000 annual deaths from the disease.

5. Smoking, Chronic Bronchitis, and Emphysema

Chronic bronchitis and emphysema are responsible for many deaths, especially in men, and are a major cause of sickness, absence from work and chronic disability (5. 1). Cigarette smokers are much more often affected by these diseases and more often have impaired function of the lungs than non-smokers or smokers of pipe and cigars (5. 3 to 5. 6). Their risk of dying from these conditions and the damage found in their lungs after death increase in direct relation to the number of cigarettes smoked (5. 8, 5. 9). The harm done by cigarettes is to some extent offset by the benefits from improved treatment and social environment, the combined effect being shown in recent trends of deaths from these diseases (5. 10). If smoking is given up, mild degrees of bronchitis and impairment of lung function improve rapidly, but severe damage to the lungs cannot be repaired (5. 7). There are other causes of bronchitis which act particularly on cigarette smokers (5. 14, 5. 15).

Cigarette smoking is now the most important predisposing cause of chronic bronchitis and emphysema. Much of the widespread disablement and many deaths from these diseases would be prevented if the habit were discontinued (5. 12, 5. 17).

6. Smoking and Diseases of the Heart and Blood Vessels

Coronary heart disease is responsible for about one in every three deaths in men between the ages of 35 and 64 and one in seven of deaths in women at these ages. Liability to this disease is approximately twice as great in cigarette smokers as in non-smokers, and is related to the numbers of cigarettes smoked, to inhalation, and to the age of starting to smoke (6. 1 to 6. 3). The excess risk of cigarette smokers from the disease declines steadily after cessation of smoking (6. 10, 6. 11).

Non-fatal attacks of coronary heart diesease, angina pectoris, and disease of the coronary arteries found post mortem are also related to cigarette smoking independently of other important causative factors that have to be considered (6. 4, 6. 6 and 6. 7).

Heredity may make some people both more prone to coronary disease and more liable to smoke cigarettes, but stopping smoking mitigates this dangerous combination (6. 9 to 6. 12).

Experimental evidence of the effects of cigarette smoking and of nicotine on the heart and blood shows how smoking could damage the coronary arteries and increase the chance of dying after a coronary thrombosis (6. 13 to 6. 15).

Pipe and cigar smokers have only a small increase of risk from coronary disease (6. 16).

It is concluded that cigarette smoking is an important factor in causing coronary heart disease and that the general avoidance of cigarettes would greatly diminish the number of deaths from this condition (6. 17).

Other diseases of the circulation, including arterial disease of the leg and strokes, are also related to cigarette smoking (6. 18 to 6. 20).

7. Smoking and Other Conditions

Mothers who smoke during pregnancy tend to have smaller babies than non-smokers and may be more likely to lose their babies from abortion, still-births and deaths in the first days of life (7. 1 to 7. 5).

Cancers of the mouth, larynx and oesophagus are more frequent in smokers of all kinds of tobacco than in non-smokers. Cancers of the bladder and pancreas are commoner in cigarette smokers than in non-smokers (7. 6 to 7. 9).

Smoking does not appear to cause gastric or duodenal ulcers but it delays their healing, so that they are more persistent and more often fatal in smokers than in non-smokers (7. 10 to 7. 16).

Cigarette smokers are more liable than non-smokers to develop tuberculosis of the lungs. This may be due to their greater consumption of alcohol (7. 17).

Smokers are more prone to accidents than are non-smokers. Fires traced to smoking are responsible for great economic loss and some 100 deaths every year in Great Britain (7. 18).

Smoking may enhance the risk of some rare forms of blindness (7. 19).

Cirrhosis of the liver, due to heavy drinking, is associated with smoking because most heavy drinkers smoke (7. 21).

Diseases of the teeth and gums are more frequent in smokers than in non-smokers (7. 22), who incidentally tend to be heavier. Those who give up smoking often put on a lot of weight, but this does not counteract the benefits to health otherwise gained (7. 23 to 7. 25).

Smokers have impaired athletic fitness compared with non-smokers (7. 26).

8. The Smoking Habit

Most smokers begin the habit in adolescence and dependence is soon established. The reasons for this are complex. In some, satisfaction of inner needs, and in others social factors seem to be most important. Smokers tend to differ from non-smokers in personality and social environment. Dependence appears to be due to the action of nicotine (8. 5 to 8. 14).

Reasons for giving up smoking are also complex: expense and effects on health predominate. The influence of family, friends, and associates is also important. Withdrawal effects are often reported but are not usually prolonged. More effective public information about the effects and consequences of smoking might persuade many to give it up—especially if there were less social acceptance of smoking. Dependent smokers may need the help of new techniques which should be developed by research in special smoking-control clinics (8. 15 to 8. 21).

9. Prevention of Diseases due to Smoking

The reality of the psychological and social benefits of smoking is suggested by the world-wide growth of the habit, but they are outweighed by the harm done to health and preventive measures are now essential. Every effort must be made to encourage people not to smoke cigarettes and at the same time to develop less dangerous products for those who cannot abstain (9. 1 to 9. 6).

Although most smokers know about the danger of the habit they reject its relevance to themselves. They must be convinced of the dangerous effect of cigarette smoking on health (9. 7 to 9. 11).

Doctors should abstain from smoking and take every opportunity to urge their patients to follow their example. Medical students should be instructed about the effects of smoking and their responsibilities in this matter must be brought home to them (9. 12 to 9. 18).

The public too should be more thoroughly informed of the dangers of smoking and the Government should consult the Broadcasting Authorities and newspaper industry on how to achieve this (9. 19 to 9. 21).

Better means of educating children about smoking must be developed. Teachers should set an example to their pupils. Regulations forbidding the sale of cigarettes to children should be strengthened and cigarette vending machines should be removed from public places (9. 22 to 9. 26).

Advertisements of cigarettes and gift coupon schemes should be prohibited (9. 27 to 9. 30).

More restrictions on smoking in public transport and places of entertainment should be enforced (9. 31).

Employers' organisations and Trade Unions should agree on wider restrictions of smoking at work (9. 32).

Life insurance companies should consider reduced premiums to non-smokers (9. 33).

Warning notices should be printed on packets of cigarettes and, if they are allowed to continue, on cigarette advertisements (9. 34, 9. 35).

More effective techniques for helping unwilling smokers to stop must be developed in special research clinics, and when this has been done smoking-control clinics should be established in hospitals, health departments, factories, and offices (9. 36, 9. 37).

Pipes and cigars appear to do little harm to health. It is likely that cigarette smokers who change over to these would benefit. Since there is evidence that cigarettes with a lower content of nicotine and tar may be less dangerous, the amounts of these in all marketed brands should be published and a public statement made on the possible effects on health of smoking them. The Government should consider imposing statutory upper limits to the nicotine and tar content of cigarettes. The Medical Research Council should consult with the tobacco industry with regard to tests of cigarettes which are likely to be less hazardous and should conduct research to determine the effects on health of smoking such cigarettes (9. 38 to 9. 46).

Meanwhile those who continue to smoke cigarettes should be encouraged to:
    smoke fewer cigarettes,
    inhale less,
    smoke less of each cigarette,
    take fewer puffs from each cigarette,
    take the cigarette out of the mouth between puffs,
    smoke brands with low nicotine and tar content (9. 47).

The Government must look beyond an easy source of revenue to the reality of the injurious effects of cigarettes on the health and economy of the country. Differential taxation of different types of tobacco should be imposed to discourage more hazardous forms of smoking. An official inquiry should be made into the economic consequences of present smoking habits and of the results of a general reduction in cigarette smoking (9. 48 to 9. 51).

Success in the prevention of diseases caused by smoking can be achieved, but only if the attack is effectively organised and made on many fronts. The goal is the preservation of the lives and health of thousands of smokers who would otherwise continue year after year to become ill and to die before their time (9. 52 to 9. 54).

Smoking and Health Now

Smoking and Health Now

A NEW REPORT AND SUMMARY
ON SMOKING AND ITS EFFECTS
ON HEALTH FROM THE ROYAL COLLEGE
OF PHYSICIANS OF LONDON

LONDON
PITMAN MEDICAL AND SCIENTIFIC
PUBLISHING CO. LTD.

First Published 1971

PITMAN MEDICAL AND SCIENTIFIC PUBLISHING
COMPANY LIMITED
31 Fitzroy Square, London, W1

Associated Companies
SIR ISAAC PITMAN AND SONS LIMITED
Pitman House, Parker Street, Kingsway,
London, WC2
P.O. Box 6038, Portal Street, Nairobi, Kenya

SIR ISAAC PITMAN (AUST.) PTY. LTD
Pitman House, Bouverie Street, Carlton,
Victoria 3053, Australia

PITMAN PUBLISHING CORPORATION S.A. LTD
P.O. Box 9898, Johannesburg, S. Africa

PITMAN PUBLISHING CORPORATION
20 East 46th Street, New York, NY10017

SIR ISAAC PITMAN (CANADA) LTD
Pitman House, 381–383 Church Street, Toronto 3

THE COPP CLARK PUBLISHING COMPANY
517 Wellington Street, Toronto 2B

1SBN 0 272 76048 x

Printed in Great Britain by Staples Printers Limited, at their Rochester,
Kent, establishment

21 3455 11

Contents

Preface

In April 1959 the Royal College of Physicians of London set up a Committee to:

> 'Report on the question of smoking and atmospheric pollution in relation to carcinoma of the lung and other illnesses.'

The Committee decided that although the effects of air pollution and smoking might be interrelated the preventive measures required were so different that the two hazards should be considered separately. The first report, *Smoking and Health*, was published in 1962. The Committee has now produced a completely new report which has been approved by the Council on behalf of the College. *Smoking and Health Now* is based on the most recent information available. It is an up to date companion of the report *Air Pollution and Health* published earlier in 1970.

The composition of the Committee is as follows:
Sir Charles Dodds (President and Chairman till 1966)
Lord Rosenheim (President and Chairman from 1966)

Sir Aubrey Lewis	Dr J. N. Morris
Dr J. G. Scadding	Dr J. C. Gilson
Dr H. A. Clegg (co-opted 1969)	Dr P. J. Lawther
Sir Francis Avery Jones	Dr D. D. Reid
Dr N. C. Oswald	Dr L. H. Capel

Dr C. M. Fletcher (Hon. Secretary)
Sir Kenneth Robson (Registrar)
Mr G. M. G. Tibbs (Secretary of the College)

The Committee wishes to acknowledge its indebtedness to Mr G. F. Todd of the Tobacco Research Council for many detailed and critical comments.

1 *Introduction*

1. 1   In 1962 the Royal College of Physicians reported that diseases associated with cigarette smoking caused so many deaths that they presented the most challenging of all opportunities for preventive medicine [15]. The challenge remains. The total number of deaths attributable to cigarette smoking rises year by year and is likely to continue to do so unless there are radical changes in smoking habits.

1. 2   The suffering and shortening of life resulting from smoking cigarettes have become increasingly clear as the evidence accumulates. Cigarette smoking is now as important a cause of death as were the great epidemic diseases such as typhoid, cholera, and tuberculosis that affected previous generations in this country. Once the causes of these had been established they were gradually brought under control. Preventive measures have virtually abolished typhoid and cholera in developed countries, and since effective drugs have been used, the number of deaths from tuberculosis has been dramatically reduced. But despite all the publicity on the dangers of cigarette smoking people seem unwilling to accept the facts and many of those who do are unwilling or unable to act upon them.

1. 3   The Government, although stating in 1962 that they accepted the evidence on the dangers of cigarette smoking, have taken no effective action to curtail the habit. Promotion of cigarette sales continues unabated, and the problem of preventing smoking has attracted little research. In this second College Report on Smoking and Health the evidence, old and new, on the effects of smoking is summarised, and proposals are made for action which might at first contain and ultimately end the present holocaust—a reasonable word to describe an annual death toll of some 27,500 in men and

women aged 35–64 from the burning of tobacco (Appendix B, p. 145).

History of Smoking [12]

1. 4   Spanish explorers of America introduced pipe smoking to western civilisation early in the sixteenth century. English explorers brought it to England, and by 1590 sufficient quantities were being imported for the Queen to impose the first import duty of 2d a pound. It is remarkable that tobacco should have become popular so quickly among people unaccustomed to it, particularly since the early tobaccos produced rank smoke with a much higher nicotine content than modern smokers would relish. Jean Nicot, French Ambassador to Lisbon, after whom nicotine was named, recommended tobacco for its medicinal value. But it soon became the subject of acute controversy. It was praised both as a restorative and as a prophylactic against many ills and condemned as a noxious vice, in particular by James I in his famous *Counterblaste to Tobacco*. This controversy has continued almost unabated ever since, but, until comparatively recently, with no valid evidence on either side.

1. 5   Throughout the seventeenth century consumption of tobacco in England rose steadily, mostly in the form of pipe smoking, but it was also chewed and snuffed. Towards the end of the century snuff-taking in fashionable circles largely replaced smoking, but the mass of the people continued to smoke pipes. Cigars were introduced at the beginning of the nineteenth century but were never as popular in Britain as on the Continent. Cigarettes were first made in the mid-eighteenth century, in Brazil, and were introduced from there to Spain. The habit of smoking them appears to have been brought to Britain by troops returning from the Crimean War. The production of milder tobaccos in Virginia, the development of the briar pipe in 1860, and increasing prosperity were followed by a further steady rise in consumption of tobacco throughout the nineteenth century.

Recent Smoking Habits [19]

1. 6   In Britain, cigarettes began to be popular among men

only at the beginning of the present century, since when they have steadily tended to replace other forms of smoking (Figure 1. 1). Women began to smoke cigarettes during and after the First World War and rarely smoke anything else. The increasing consumption of cigarettes among women has run, some twenty years later, roughly parallel to that of men.

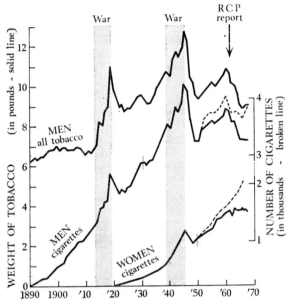

Figure 1. 1 *Tobacco consumption in the United Kingdom from 1890–1968.*
This figure gives the annual consumption of tobacco in pounds per adult (aged 16 and over). Ten pounds of tobacco is equivalent to about 5,500 cigarettes which, if consumed in one year, would mean smoking an average of about 15 cigarettes daily. The decline of tobacco smoking by men since 1960 has been due in part to the growing use of filter-tipped cigarettes, which contain less tobacco than non-filter cigarettes, but there has been a small decrease in numbers of cigarettes smoked by men (broken line). The steady trend in the growth of cigarette smoking by men has been interrupted by sharp peaks during both wars. They have smoked more cigarettes than tobacco in other forms, so that there has been a steady decrease in the use of the latter. Women hardly smoked at all until after the First World War. Fewer of them smoke cigarettes than men, but the proportion of women who smoke is still increasing.

At all ages, however, fewer women smoke than men (Figure 1. 2), and on average those who do, smoke less; they also begin at a later age and inhale less. Of those who in 1968 had ever been regular smokers, 83 per cent of men but only 60 per cent of women had begun before the age of 20: 53 per cent of women smokers compared with 77 per cent of men said they inhaled more than a little.

1. 7   After publication of the first College Report, *Smoking and Health*, in 1962, the number of cigarettes smoked by men dropped sharply but it subsequently rose gradually to a

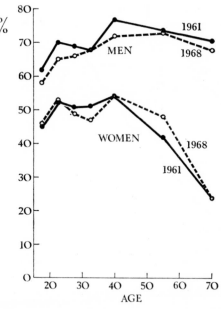

Figure 1. 2   *Percentage of men and women who smoked in 1961 and 1968.* The figure shows the percentage of smokers in men and women according to their ten-year age groups. The year 1961 was the last before publication of the first College Report, *Smoking and Health*, which resulted in wide publicity about the hazards of smoking. Since 1961 there has been a small decline in the percentage of men of all ages who smoke. There has been no change in the number of women under the age of 40 who smoke; at older ages there has been a slight increase. This is due chiefly to the younger women who have been heavier smokers moving into the older age groups.

figure only just below that of 1961. The upward trend of numbers of cigarettes smoked by women continued. Since 1961 the percentage of men at all ages smoking has fallen slightly (Figure 1. 2). This decrease has occurred chiefly in men in the professional and skilled occupations (social classes I, II and III). There has been no change in the smoking habits of men in partially-skilled occupations (social classes IV and V). The percentage of women who smoke has declined recently in social classes I to IV but has increased in social class V; and those who smoke are now smoking more. There is some uncertainty about changes in smoking habits among boys and girls. The Tobacco Research Council (TRC), interviewing children in their homes, often in the

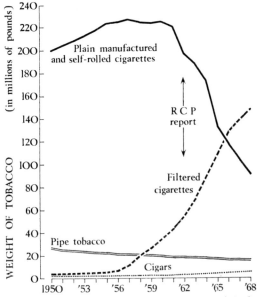

Figure 1. 3 *Changes in consumption of various tobacco goods in the past fifteen years.* There has been a steady decline in the numbers of plain cigarettes and a corresponding increase in the numbers of filter-tipped cigarettes smoked. The publication of the first College Report, *Smoking and Health*, had no effect on this trend. There has been a steady decline in the use of pipe tobacco. Six times more cigars were smoked in 1968 than in 1956, but only 1·5 per cent of all tobacco smoked is now cigar tobacco.

presence of the parents, found that between the years 1961 and 1968 there was a small reduction in smoking by boys [19]. But a survey using confidential questionnaires in 1966 reported no significant change in smoking by boys since 1961 [2]. The TRC figures indicate a steady rise in smoking by girls since 1961.

1. 8   In the USA recent trends have been more favourable. Cigarette smoking reached its maximum in 1964, the year in which the Surgeon-General published his Report on Smoking and Health. Consumption of cigarettes per capita then levelled off and began to decline [7]. One in three of men

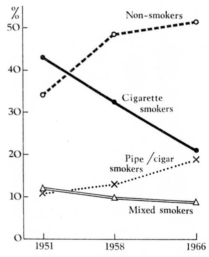

Figure 1. 4   *Changes in doctors' smoking habits 1951–1966.* This figure illustrates changes in the smoking habits of those doctors who replied to questionnaires in 1951, 1958, and 1966 [5a, 5b]. Although there were rather more non-smokers and fewer cigarette smokers in this sample than among doctors as a whole, the changes during this period may be taken to represent changes that occurred generally among doctors. The proportion of non-smokers rose and the proportion of cigarette smokers declined even more, because some cigarette smokers switched to smoking pipes and cigars. The proportion smoking cigars and pipes as well as cigarettes declined slightly. There was little corresponding change in the smoking habits of the general population during the same period.

and one in four of women in America who were smoking in 1966 had stopped by July 1970 [20].

1. 9 During the past fifteen years there has been a steady change from plain to filter-tipped cigarettes (Figure 1. 3). In 1950, only one per cent of all cigarettes smoked were filter-tipped; now nearly three-quarters are. This change began before any public statement had been made about the risks of cigarette smoking and there was no noticeable alteration in the rate of switching to filters after the first College Report was published in 1962. Although about one in every four smokers believes that filter-tips reduce the risk of cancer and other diseases, the majority give cheapness, convenience, and

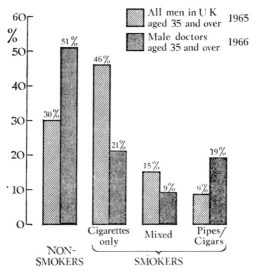

Figure 1. 5 *Smoking habits of male doctors aged 35 and over compared with other men of the same ages in the United Kingdom in 1965–1966.* There were many more non-smokers among doctors than the general public, and only half as many cigarette smokers. There were fewer mixed smokers (those who smoked cigarettes as well as pipes or cigars) so that the total percentage of doctors who smoked any cigarettes was 30 compared with 61 among all men. More doctors than other men smoked only pipes and cigars. The figures for doctors are based upon a survey of doctors carried out in 1966 [5*b*], those for men of the same age in 1965 are taken from Research Paper No. 1 of the Tobacco Research Council [19].

enjoyment as reasons for preferring them [11]. Six times as
many cigars are now smoked as in 1956, but only 1·5 per cent
of all tobacco is smoked in this form. A steady decline in the
smoking of pipe tobacco has continued.

Reduction of Cigarette Smoking by Doctors and Others

1. 10   Doctors' smoking habits were recorded in 1951, 1958,
and 1966 [5a, 5b] and are shown in Figure 1. 4. Between
1951 (when evidence of the risks of cigarette smoking was
first recognised by most doctors) and 1966, the proportion
of non-smokers rose from 34 per cent to 51 per cent; that of
cigarette smokers fell from 43 per cent to 21 per cent; while
the percentage of smokers of only pipes or cigars rose from
11 to 19. There was a slight fall in the numbers of mixed
smokers. There is a striking contrast between the smoking
habits of doctors and those of other men over the age of 35,
among whom there was little change over this period. In
1966, 46 per cent were still cigarette smokers, 15 per cent
mixed smokers, 9 per cent smokers of pipes and cigars
only, while 30 per cent were non-smokers (Figure 1. 5).
Similar recent changes in the smoking habits of doctors have
been reported from Canada [14], New Zealand [8], and the
USA [9, 16]. Although doctors commonly say they have
stopped smoking because of its immediate effects on their
health, they refer to remoter health risks as their reason more
often than do members of the general public [6]. It was,
however, found in 1963 that there had been as great a reduction of cigarette smoking among non-medical as among
medical graduate staff of the University of Edinburgh [10].
This may be just one aspect of the general falling off in
cigarette smoking by the professional, clerical, and skilled
working classes [19], who are more aware of the risks and
readier to avoid them.

Tobacco Advertising

1. 11   Substantial competition between the major manufacturers dates chiefly from 1955, when leaf supplies became
more plentiful after post-war scarcity. Since then, expenditure
on advertising of other goods has not quite doubled, while

expenditure on tobacco advertising has more than trebled. After the end of July 1965, advertising of cigarettes was banned on television, and subsequently there was a moderate rise (greater than the increase in sales) in advertising of pipe tobacco and cigars. There were few gift-coupon schemes till 1963, but expenditure on this form of sales promotion is now larger than that devoted to direct advertising (Table 1. 1 and Figure 1. 6).

1. 12   In 1962, the British tobacco manufacturers voluntarily adopted a code that excluded any cigarette advertisements

TABLE 1. 1

UK expenditure on sales promotion of cigarettes, tobaccos, and cigars, 1955–1968
(figures in £ million)

	Advertisements						Gift Coupons		Grand Total	
	Medium									
Year	Press	Posters	TV	Cinema	Actual Total	Adjusted Total*	Actual Total	Adjusted Total*	Actual Total	Adjusted Total*
1955	1·7	0·6	—	0·1	2·4	3·0	—	—	2·4	3·0
1956	2·1	0·6	0·4	0·1	3·2	3·8	—	—	3·2	3·8
1957	2·5	0·7	1·3	0·3	4·8	5·6	—	—	4·8	5·6
1958	2·6	0·7	1·9	0·2	5·4	6·2	—	—	5·4	6·2
1959	2·6	0·7	2·9	0·2	6·4	7·1	—	—	6·4	7·1
1960	3·6	0·9	4·2	0·4	9·1	9·1	—	—	9·1	9·1
1961	3·7	1·3	5·3	0·3	10·6	9·5	—	—	10·6	9·5
1962	5·3	1·7	5·8	0·3	13·1	11·3	—	—	13·1	11·3
1963	5·8	2·0	6·2	0·5	14·5	12·2	8·8	7·4	23·3	19·6
1964	7·7	2·2	8·1	0·5	18·5	14·4	10·3	8·0	28·8	22·4
1965	10·4	3·1	7·0	0·6	21·1	16·3	13·0	10·0	34·1	26·3
1966	10·3	3·2	2·5	0·6	16·6	13·1	24·4	19·3	41·0	32·4
1967	8·5	2·7	2·9	0·2	14·3	10·8	33·2	25·1	47·5	35·9
1968	11·0	3·0	2·8	0·2	17·0	12·2	35·2	25·3	52·2	37·5

* Adjusted for increased costs based on 1960.

Note The Tobacco manufacturers state that there are important differences between advertising expenditure and coupon trading which make it quite unjustifiable to add the two together. Cigarette advertising is entirely under the control of the manufacturer and is incurred solely in aid of inter-brand competition. In contrast, the cost of coupon trading is not under the control of the manufacturers but is dictated by the free choice made by the smoker to purchase a brand containing a coupon to be redeemed at a later date for goods or cash. The increase in recent years in the total monetary exchange value of coupons simply reflects the increasing popularity of coupon brands.

which over-emphasised the pleasures of smoking; featured conventional heroes of the young; appealed to manliness, romance, or social success; or implied greater safety of any brand [17]. Some advertisements of this kind, aimed at young people, continue to appear for a few brands of cigarettes. Despite the prohibition of television advertising, the total expenditure on advertisements in 1968 amounted to £17,000,000 and on coupon schemes to over £35,000,000, making a total of £52,000,000 (*see* Table 1. 1). In 1966 the

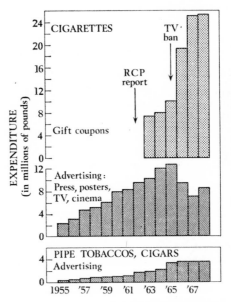

Figure 1. 6   *Expenditure on advertising tobacco goods in the press, on television, and on gift coupons in the United Kingdom 1955–1968 (adjusted to 1960 costs).* Much of the increase in expenditure on advertising between 1955 and 1965 was due to television cigarette advertising. After the ban on television advertising was imposed in 1965, the expenditure on advertising cigarettes fell and there was a simultaneous rise in expenditure on advertising of pipe tobaccos and cigars. Expenditure on gift coupon schemes has expanded rapidly since 1963. The trend of increasing expenditure on advertising cigarettes was uninfluenced by the widespread publicity about the hazards of cigarette smoking which followed the publication of the report in 1962 of the Royal College of Physicians, *Smoking and Health*.

Minister of Health approached the tobacco manufacturers and secured a six-months' voluntary agreement to restrict expenditure on advertising of cigarettes, but during 1967 the restriction broke down under the stress of competition between the manufacturers, especially in relation to gift-coupon schemes. The effect of advertising on cigarette consumption is discussed in paragraphs 9. 27 and 9. 28.

Research

1. 13   The Medical Research Council has sponsored much research into the effects of smoking on health including the important study of British doctors by Doll and Hill [5*a*], but it has taken little action in the field of prevention. In November 1966 the Council, with the Ministry of Health and Social Science Research Council, held a conference on the possibilities of research into smoking habituation, but the Council received very few applications for research grants in this field until 1969, when support was given for two studies of methods of giving up smoking. The Council's Committee on General Epidemiology has now set up a Working Party to advise on research into problems of altering public attitudes to smoking, into consequent changes of smoking habits, and their effects on health.

1. 14   The British tobacco manufacturers have supported research into smoking and health since 1954, when they gave £250,000 to the Medical Research Council. In 1956 they set up their own Tobacco Research Council (TRC). This has supported research on smoking and health by many independent organisations and individuals [18], and this includes epidemiological, clinical, and laboratory studies of chest and heart diseases associated with smoking, and surveys on smoking habits [19]. In 1962, work began in the TRC's own laboratories at Harrogate. There the research includes animal studies related to the role of cigarette smoking in lung cancer, on the working hypothesis that cigarette smoke affects the respiratory epithelium by direct contact, and pharmacological studies of nicotine. The Tobacco Research Council's annual contribution to such research is about £1,000,000 per annum. In addition, the manufacturers

spend a similar amount on research in their own laboratories and elsewhere.

Action by Government and Other Authorities

1. 15   After publication of the College Report in 1962, Government spokesmen accepted its findings without dissent, but action was limited to issuing posters and pamphlets about smoking by the Ministry of Health and the Central Council for Health Education. In 1964, at the request of the Ministry of Health, the Social Survey investigated smoking habits and attitudes among schoolboys [2], medical students [1], and the general public [11]. The Press has given publicity to the forthright statements on the dangers of cigarette smoking made by the Chief Medical Officer of the Ministry of Health in his annual reports. Posters were prepared and widely displayed, and three films made for schoolchildren. Another approach was by special posters and anti-smoking strip cartoons in children's magazines. Three one-minute films have been produced for showing by the BBC and ITA. The total expenditure by the newly established Health Education Council on these activities has risen to £100,000 per annum, while £52 million were spent in 1968 on promoting cigarette sales. The Ministry of Transport, faced with deaths from road accidents far fewer than those due to smoking, spend £1·3 million annually on public education on road safety.

1. 16   In January 1967, the Minister of Health was asked about restrictions of smoking in places of public entertainment. He said the Government felt 'that it would not be appropriate to take powers for compulsory restrictions on smoking in such places', and smoking continues to be permitted in most of them. There has been a slight increase in non-smoking accommodation on some main line services and in London Underground trains, in contrast to the prohibition of smoking in the underground trains of Moscow, New York, and Paris. In an answer to a question in November 1967, the Minister said: 'there is some reluctance to impose further restrictions on smoking which may prove unpopular with the public'. Yet the Social Survey found that only a minority

(40 per cent) of the public opposed a ban on smoking in buses and only one in five (22 per cent) objected to an increase in non-smoking compartments in trains [11].

1. 17 In May 1963 the Ministry of Health issued a circular requesting the restriction of smoking in hospitals, especially in out-patient departments. It was recognised that a total ban on smoking by in-patients could not be imposed, but there 'should be no encouragement to smoke', and smoking should be limited to day rooms or to particular wards and particular times of the day. Cigarettes should not be on display for sale. In January 1967, an inquiry showed that nearly all hospitals had imposed restrictions but that 'there was room for further restrictions on smoking at some hospitals'.

1. 18 In March 1970, a Senior Medical Officer was appointed in the Department of Health and Social Security to co-ordinate work of various departments on smoking and health. Eventually a unit with a full-time staff may be developed for this purpose, as has been done in the US Department of Health, Education and Welfare.

1. 19 A few hospitals and local authorities have organised anti-smoking clinics to help those who wish to stop smoking, mostly on the initiative of individual doctors. The six-month success rate reported from these clinics varied between 10 per cent and 70 per cent with an average of about 30 per cent [4]. A conference of doctors in charge of these clinics held at the Ministry of Health in October 1965 recommended a uniform system of recording that would facilitate comparative trials of different techniques; but no action was taken, and many of these clinics have been discontinued.

1. 20 It seems that Ministers, while accepting the evidence that cigarette smoking is dangerous to health, are guided in their actions by the view that the risks are regrettable but inevitable consequences of a habit which they believe to be an essential source of revenue. A former Minister in a Conservative Government, once Minister of Health, wrote in 1966: 'Smokers, mainly cigarette smokers, contribute some £1,000 million yearly to the Exchequer . . . and no-one knows better than the Government that they simply can't afford to lose so much' [13]. In 1969, in reply to a letter from

a colleague, a Labour Minister expounded this view in greater detail. He wrote:

> The introduction of a meaningful differential tax on cigarettes would be bound to have a seriously detrimental effect on the total revenue obtainable from tobacco. The object of such a tax would be to reduce cigarette smoking, and pipes and cigars would not be acceptable alternatives for many cigarette smokers. Furthermore, apart from those who gave up smoking altogether, cigarette smokers who switched to cigars would consume less tobacco in proportion to their expenditure and those who switched to pipe tobacco would consume less tobacco in proportion to the time spent in smoking. Thus the capacity of the tobacco duty to produce revenue would be eroded.

With neither of these statements was there any mention of the human suffering associated with this source of revenue or of the economic loss due to illness and shortening of life which cigarette smoking causes [3] (Appendix A).

1. 21   It is hoped that this second Report of the Royal College of Physicians, by its renewed presentation of the evidence of the dangers of cigarette smoking, will at last arouse the public conscience and persuade the Government to take effective preventive measures against a deadly habit.

REFERENCES

1. BYNNER, J. M. (1967). *Medical Students' Attitudes towards Smoking*. A report on a survey carried out for the Ministry of Health. SS 382. HMSO, London.

2. BYNNER, J. M. (1969). *The Young Smoker*. A study of smoking among schoolboys carried out for the Ministry of Health. SS 383. HMSO, London.

3. COLE, H. (1965). *Common Sense about Smoking*. 'The Economic Effects.' Penguin Books, Harmondsworth, Middx.

4. CRUIKSHANK, A. (1964). Ministry of Health Report to conference on smoking clinics. October 1964, unpublished.

5a. DOLL, R., and HILL, A. B. (1964). 'Mortality in relation to smoking: ten years' observations of British doctors.' *Brit. med. J.*, **1**, 1399 and 1460.

5b. DOLL, R., and PIKE, M. C. (1970). Personal communication.

6. FLETCHER, C. M., and DOLL, R. (1969). 'A survey of doctors' attitudes to smoking.' *Br. J. prev. soc. Med.*, **23**, 145.

7. FLETCHER, C. M., and HORN, D. (1970). 'Smoking and Health'. *WHO Chronicle*, **24**, 345.

8. GARDINER, C. E., and TAYLOR, C. N. D. (1964). *Smoking Habits of New Zealand Doctors*. New Zealand Dept. of Health Special Report No. 16.

9. GARFINKEL, L. (1967). 'Changes in cigarette smoking habits among physicians 1959–65.' *C.A.* (N.Y.), **17**, 193.

10. LYNCH, G. W. (1963). 'Smoking habits of medical and non-medical university staff.' *Br. med. J.*, **1**, 852.

11. McKENNELL, A. C., and THOMAS, R. K. (1967). *Adults' and Adolescents' Smoking Habits and Attitudes*. A report on a survey carried out for the Ministry of Health. SS 353/B HMSO, London.

12. MACKENZIE, C. (1957). *Sublime Tobacco*. Chatto and Windus, London.

13. MACLEOD, IAIN (1966). *Daily Mail*, December 13.

14. PHILLIPS, A. J., and TAYLOR, R.M. (1968). 'Smoking habits of physicians in Canada.' *Can. med. Ass. J.*, **99**, 955.

15. ROYAL COLLEGE OF PHYSICIANS (1962). *Smoking and Health*. Pitman Medical, London.

16. SNEGIREFF, L. S., and LOMBARD, O. M. (1959). 'Smoking habits of Massachusetts physicians.' Five-year follow-up study (1954–59). *New Engl. J. Med.*, **261**, 603.

17. TOBACCO ADVISORY COMMITTEE (1964). *Code of Cigarette Advertising Practice*. Tobacco Advisory Committee, London SW1.

18. TOBACCO RESEARCH COUNCIL (1967). *Review of Activities* 1963–1966. Tobacco Research Council, London SW1.

19. TODD, G. F. (1969). *Statistics of Smoking in the United Kingdom*. Tobacco Research Council, Research Paper No. 1, Fifth edit.

20. HORN, D. Address given at National Council of Smoking and Health, San Diego, Calif., September 9th, 1970.

2. 1   Pearl, in 1938 [7], was the first to attempt an informed comparison between death rates* of large numbers of smokers and non-smokers, and found that heavy smokers had higher death rates than non-smokers, particularly before the age of 45. His report was widely criticised, and in 1948 an editorial in the *Journal of the American Medical Association* [5] observed that, 'extensive scientific studies have proved that smoking in moderation by those for whom tobacco is not especially con-tra-indicated does not appreciably shorten life'. Pearl's find-ings have now been confirmed and extended by prospective studies in which the smoking habits of large numbers of smokers and non-smokers have been determined and the number and causes of death occurring among them recorded in subsequent years. These have provided detailed assessment of the diminished expectation of life of smokers according to the amount and type of smoking.

Death Rates in Relation to Smoking Habits
2. 2   Large surveys of this sort have been carried out on British doctors [2], on American veterans [6], on men and women in twenty-five States in the USA [3] (the largest of them all), and on Canadian veterans [1]. These four investi-gations all tell the same story. Cigarette smokers have shorter lives than non-smokers, and heavy cigarette smokers have shorter lives than lighter smokers. Those who smoke only pipes or cigars have death rates only a little higher than those of non-smokers (Figure 2. 1): most men who smoke only pipes or cigars are moderate smokers who do not inhale, and they

---

* A death rate is a measure of the risk that an individual in a defined group has of dying in the course of one year.

have death rates similar to non-smokers; but the minority who smoke heavily (ten or more cigars or twenty or more pipes daily) and inhale, incur the same risk to life as do lighter cigarette smokers [3, 6].

2. 3   The percentage increase in death rates of cigarette smokers is higher at younger than at older ages, but the total number of excess deaths is higher at older ages. Thus in the largest American study [3], from which Figure 2. 2 is de-

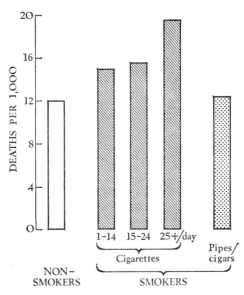

Figure 2. 1   *Number of deaths each year per thousand in male British doctors according to their smoking habits* [2]. The annual risk of dying (standardised for age differences) is greater in those who smoke cigarettes than in non-smokers and the risk increases with the number of cigarettes smoked. The relatively small difference between those smoking 1–14/day and 15–24/day may be due to some heavier smokers who were suffering symptoms from their smoking having reduced their cigarette consumption shortly before the beginning of the survey. These, previously heavy smoking doctors, would be included in the lighter group, for the smoking habits recorded were those reported at the beginning of the survey. Men who were smoking only pipes and cigars have a risk of dying almost exactly the same as that of non-smokers para 2. 2).

rived, the number of deaths per thousand each year in men aged 35 to 44 is 2·1 in non-smokers and 5·5 in smokers of forty or more cigarettes a day. The rate is thus two and a half times higher in the heavy smokers, but because death rates at this age are low there are only 3·4 extra deaths per thousand each year. In men aged 65 to 74, the respective rates are 31·2 for non-smokers and 56·4 for the heaviest smokers. The heavier smokers' rate is less than twice that of non-smokers, but there are 25·2 extra deaths per thousand each year. Death rates for the heaviest smokers are similar to those of non-smokers ten years older.

2. 4   The earlier in life cigarette smoking begins the bigger the risk. Those who inhale run a greater risk to life than those

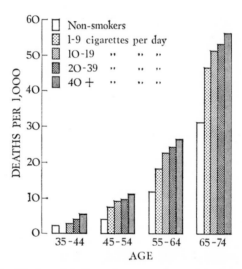

Figure 2. 2   Number of deaths each year per thousand in American men at various ages according to numbers of cigarettes smoked [3]. Death-rates naturally increase with age. Smoking causes a greater proportionate increase in annual death-rates in younger than in older men, but the risk of smoking is really more serious in the older men because their death rates are so much higher. It is more dangerous nearly to double a large risk than to raise a small risk nearly threefold. The heavier smokers have a risk of dying each year which is similar to that of non-smokers ten years older. There were too few deaths in smokers of 1–9 cigarettes per day aged 35–44 to provide a reliable figure.

who do not, but the latter have a greater risk than those who do not smoke at all [3, 6].

Excess of Deaths in Cigarette Smokers in the United Kingdom

2. 5   The total number of excess deaths each year in male smokers compared with male non-smokers in the United Kingdom may be estimated from the prospective study of British doctors [2]. From this source it is estimated that in 1968 in Britain there were some 31,000 more deaths in men aged 35 to 64 than would have occurred if they had all been non-smokers, and that some 20,000 of these deaths were due to smoking. Another estimate gives some 27,500 deaths due to smoking in men and women aged 35 to 64 in 1968 (Appendix B).

Risk to Individual Cigarette Smokers

2. 6   Statistics of excess deaths among cigarette smokers as a group may not give the individual smoker a clear idea of how much worse off he is than his non-smoking contemporaries. Table 2. 1, derived from the study of British doctors, shows the chances that an average cigarette smoker who consumes various numbers of cigarettes per day has of dying within the next ten years, calculated for four decades between the ages of 35 and 74. The significance of these figures may be illustrated in terms of a lottery by supposing that for each ten-year period a man draws a ticket from a box containing one ticket marked 'death' among a number of blanks. If he

TABLE 2. 1

Fractional risk of dying from all causes, in decades from age 35 to age 74
(Based on death rates in British doctors 1951–65 (2a, 2b)*

Decade	Non-smokers	Smokers of:		
		1–14/day	15–24/day	25 or more/day
35–44	1 in 75	1 in 47	1 in 50	1 in 22
45–54	1 in 27	1 in 19	1 in 13	1 in 10
55–64	1 in 9	1 in 6	1 in 5	1 in 4
65–74	1 in 3	1 in 2	1 in 2	1 in 2

* *See* para B. 3, page 145, for adjustment of doctors' rates to the general population.

draws the marked ticket he dies within the next ten years. The ratios in Table 2. 1 indicate the number of tickets among which the one marked ticket is placed. Thus, for a non-smoker aged 35, there is one marked ticket for the next ten years in a box of 75 tickets but for a heavy smoker of this age the marked ticket is one among 22.

2. 7   Another point worth stressing is the chance of survival

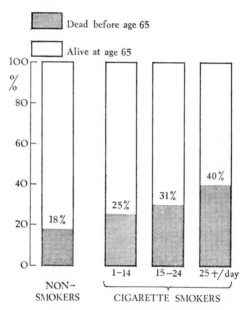

Figure 2. 3   *Proportion of men aged 35 who will die before they reach the age of 65 according to their smoking habits.* These figures, derived from the survey of British doctors [2a] show the chances a man aged 35 has of dying before the age of 65 if he is either a non-smoker or smokes various numbers of cigarettes. Only 18 per cent of the non-smokers but 25 per cent of the lighter smokers, and 31 per cent of the moderate smokers and 40 per cent of the heavier smokers (2 in 5) will die before they are 65. Of those who do reach this age more of the smokers than of the non-smokers are already disabled by chronic disease of the heart or lungs and the years of retirement will be fewer for the smokers than for the non-smokers (*see* Table 2. 2). The chances of the lighter smokers may be better than those shown because this group probably includes some formerly heavy smokers who have reduced their smoking due to illness (*see* note under Table 2. 1).

to the customary retiring age of 65. Figure 2. 3, also based on the study of British doctors, shows the proportion of non-smokers and of light, moderate, and heavy smokers aged 35 who will survive to this age. The heavy smoker has a two in five chance of dying before the age of 65 while for a non-smoker the risk is only one in five. The amount by which a cigarette smoker's life is shortened at various ages, according to the number of cigarettes he smokes, was calculated for American men by Hammond [4] (Table 2. 2). This shows the average expectation of life of men smoking different quantities of cigarettes at various ages, and the number of years of life the cigarette smokers lose compared with non-smokers. Thus an average smoker of 15 cigarettes per day aged 30 will, by this estimate, expect to lose about five and a half years of life.

TABLE 2. 2

Life expectancy of American men at various ages, and 'years of life lost' by cigarette smokers [4]

Cigarettes per day	Life Expectation	Present age								
		25	30	35	40	45	50	55	60	65
0	Years expected	48·6	43·9	39·2	34·5	30·0	25·6	21·4	17·6	14·1
1–9	Years expected	44·0	39·3	34·7	30·2	25·9	21·8	17·9	14·5	11·3
	Years lost*	4·6	4·6	4·5	4·3	4·1	3·8	3·5	3·1	2·8
10–19	Years Years lost*	43·1	38·4	33·8	29·3	25·0	21·0	17·4	14·1	11·2
		5·5	5·5	5·4	5·2	5·0	4·6	4·0	3·5	2·9
20–39	Years expected	42·4	37·8	33·2	28·7	24·4	20·5	17·0	13·7	11·0
	Years lost*	6·2	6·1	6·0	5·8	5·6	5·1	4·4	3·9	3·1

* The decrease in the number of years of life lost by cigarette smokers as they get older (which may suggest that their outlook improves as they continue to smoke) is, of course, due to the shortening expectation of life. The *percentage* reduction of expectation of life gets greater with advancing age. Thus the smoker of 10–19 cigarettes per day has an expectation reduced by 11 per cent when he is 25, but by 21 per cent when he is 65.

Effect of Stopping Smoking

2. 8   The individual will also want to know whether his risk of a shortened life could be avoided by stopping smoking. Prospective studies have all shown that when cigarette smokers cease smoking the difference between their death rate and that of non-smokers decreases steadily, and after ten years' abstinence has almost disappeared (Figure 2. 4).This reduction of excess risk among those who have stopped is found at all ages.

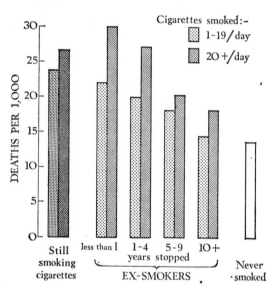

Figure 2. 4   Number of deaths each year per thousand in American men (standardised for age) who are still smoking cigarettes, who have stopped for various periods, and in those who have never smoked [3]. *The lighter smokers show a steady decline of annual death rates after stopping until, after ten years, the risk is only slightly greater than that of those who have never smoked. In the heavier smokers the increased number of deaths in the first year after stopping is probably because some have ceased smoking on account of illness; reduction of risk does not appear until five years have passed and after ten years they still have a greater risk than those who have never smoked. The reduction of the increased risk on stopping smoking is observed in older as well as in younger smokers so that except in those whose health is already seriously impaired the cigarette smoker's increased risk of dying can always be reduced by stopping smoking.*

2. 9 Between 1951 and 1965 about half of British doctors who used to smoke cigarettes stopped smoking them (para 1. 10). Many of them did this because of the evidence that it is harmful to health. A comparison of the years 1953–1957 with the years 1962–1965, shows that the death rate of the sample of doctors aged 35 to 64 fell from 853 to 747 per 100,000, a reduction of 12·4 per cent, while in the total male population of England and Wales at the same ages it fell from 994 to 965 per 100,000, a fall of only 2·9 per cent (Table 2. 3). That this contrast was due to the changes in doctors' smoking habits is indicated by the fact that for diseases which are not related to cigarette smoking the change in death

TABLE 2. 3

Changes in death rates per 100,000, standardised for age in doctors and in all men aged 35 to 64 in England and Wales 1953–1957 and 1962–1965

Cause of death	Male doctors			All men in England and Wales		
	Period		% Change	Period		% Change
	1953–57	1962–65		1953–57	1962–65	
Coronary heart diease	294	277	− 6	219	290	+32
Other cardiovascular diseases	167	157	− 6	185	152	−18
All cardiovascular diseases	461	434	− 6	404	442	+ 9
Cancer of the lung	60	37	−38	113	120	+ 6
Chronic bronchitis	18	14	−22	74	71	− 4
Major diseases related to cigarette smoking	**539**	**485**	**−10**	**591**	**633**	**+ 7**
Other cancers*	130	99	−24	152	145	− 5
Other causes*	184	163	−11	250	188	−25
All unrelated causes	**314**	**262**	**−17**	**402**	**332**	**−17**
All causes	**853**	**747**	**−12**	**993**	**966**	**− 3**

* These include a small number of deaths from cancers of mouth, throat, and oesophagus, from tuberculosis, from cirrhosis of the liver, and from peptic ulcer, which are related to cigarette smoking but make only a small contribution to the excess deaths of cigarette smokers.

rates was almost identical in both doctors and other men, while for diseases related to smoking the doctors' mortality fell by 10 per cent while the general mortality rose by 7 per cent [2a]. This change in death rate represents the prevention of premature deaths of about eighty doctors every year. The benefit that British doctors have won at the peak of their professional careers provides the strongest evidence there is of the value of giving up cigarettes.

Are the excess deaths of cigarette smokers due to smoking?

2. 10   The implication that the excess deaths of cigarette smokers are due to smoking, and would not have occurred if they had not smoked has been challenged. It has been suggested that people become habitual cigarette smokers because of inborn characteristics which are linked with a liability to die from a variety of diseases. About two-thirds of the premature deaths of smokers are due to lung cancer, chronic bronchitis, and coronary heart disease, and in later chapters evidence will be presented that most of these are due to smoking rather than to other characteristics of smokers. Strong evidence to support this conclusion is provided by the experience, just described, of those who stop smoking. If their risk were lower than that of continuing smokers because they were born with a lower risk of illness and less desire to continue smoking, their death rates would always have been lower than those of continuing smokers and would not steadily decline after stopping. A small proportion of the premature deaths of cigarette smokers are certainly due to other associated habits such as heavy drinking, but it is reasonable to conclude that most of them are due to the effects of cigarette smoking.

Disablement by Cigarette Smoking

2. 11   Cigarette smoking not only shortens life: it may also cause prolonged ill-health. While, for example, many patients recover completely from an attack of coronary disease, there are others who remain invalids after the attack. And patients who ultimately die from chronic bronchitis or emphysema

usually endure ten or more years of distressing breathlessness before they die. Cigarette smokers are also more liable than non-smokers to attacks of acute bronchitis and other chest illnesses. In Britain as many as 50 million working days may be lost to industry every year as a consequence of cigarette smoking.

Validity of the Evidence

2. 12   The investigations from which estimates of the smoker's increased risks of illness and premature death have been derived in this and other sections of this report have nearly all been carried out in various countries on people who have voluntarily agreed to participate. People who volunteer for this sort of research tend to be rather more healthy than those who do not volunteer and the total death rates of the individuals who have been studied are lower than those of the general population from which they came. It is unlikely that smoking has more effect on these volunteers than on other people, so that the magnitude of the effect of smoking on general death rates, as a whole and from individual diseases, is unlikely to have been exaggerated.

2. 13   Most of the researches have been carried out on men. Large numbers of women were included in only one of the prospective studies [3]: the findings for women were similar, but the excess mortality of women cigarette smokers was not as great. This may be partly because women tend to start smoking later in life, to smoke less, and to inhale less. But even in groups with apparently similar habits in these respects the excess mortality among women who smoke was less than that among men.

2. 14   When told of the dangers of the habit, cigarette smokers often retort that they know of heavy smokers who have remained well to a ripe old age. A simple analogy may help such smokers to understand the meaning of 'increased risk'. Not all racing motorists are killed in car crashes, but their risk is much greater than it is for the ordinary motorist. Similarly, cigarette smokers do not all die prematurely from diseases related to smoking but their chances of doing so are much greater than those of non-smokers.

Conclusion

2. 15   Cigarette smoking shortens the smoker's average life span. Stopping smoking is followed by a gradual return to the non-smoker's prospect of life. Cigarette smoking also causes increased sickness and consequent loss of work. Those who smoke cigarettes have a greatly reduced chance of surviving to retirement and a greater likelihood that, if they do survive, they may be too disabled to enjoy it. Many people look forward to some years of retirement which they will be well enough to enjoy. There is good evidence that the sooner cigarette smokers abandon the habit the better their chances are of fulfilling this hope.

REFERENCES

1. BEST, E. W. R. (1966). *A Canadian Study of Smoking and Health.* Department of National Health and Welfare, Ottawa.

2. DOLL, R., and HILL, A. B. (1964). 'Mortality in relation to smoking: ten years' observations of British doctors.' *Br. med. J.*, **1**, 1399.

2a. DOLL, R., and PIKE, M. C. (1970). Personal communication.

3. HAMMOND, E. C. (1966). 'Smoking in relation to the death rates of one million men and women.' *Natn. Cancer Inst. Monogr.*, **19**, 127.

4. HAMMOND, E. C. (1968). 'The scientific background.' World Conference on Smoking and Health, New York, 1967. *Summary of proceedings.* American Cancer Society, New York, p. 14

5. JOURNAL OF THE AMERICAN MEDICAL ASSOCIATION (1948). Editorial, **138**, 652.

6. KAHN, H. A. (1966). 'The Dorn study of smoking and mortality among US Veterans: Report on $8\frac{1}{2}$ years of observation.' *Natn. Cancer Inst. Monogr.*, **19**, 1.

7. PEARL, R. (1938). 'Tobacco smoking and longevity.' *Science*, N.Y., **87**, 216.

3 The Chemistry and Pharmacology of Tobacco Smoke

3. 1   Tobacco smoke is a mixture of gases and minute tarry droplets in which nearly one thousand compounds have been identified. Its composition varies with the type of tobacco plant from which the leaf is gathered, the way it is cured,* and the way it is smoked. The smoke that curls away from the burning ember into the surrounding air, the 'side-stream' smoke, is more concentrated than the 'main-stream' smoke. Some components of this are filtered off as it passes through the unburnt tobacco and in cigarettes it is diluted by air drawn through the paper. The smoke thus retained in the unburnt tobacco is partly redistilled when the ember reaches it, so that the smoke in each puff becomes more concentrated as smoking continues [18, 37, 56]. Cigarette paper makes an insignificant contribution to the smoke but its porosity can affect the dilution of the smoke and also the rate of burning and hence its composition [42]. The main-stream smoke of most cigarettes is faintly acid and less irritant than that of pipes, which may be acid or alkaline, or than cigar smoke, which is alkaline [47]. Cigarette smoke is the most likely to be inhaled since it is the least irritant.

3. 2   Some of the compounds in tobacco smoke act chiefly in the mouth or air passages where they are deposited.

* The species of tobacco plant used for manufacturing tobacco are hybrid and vary widely in their characteristics which are also affected by the conditions under which they are grown [62]. The leaves taken from different parts of the plant and different segments of the leaf also vary greatly in their chemical composition. There are three main procedures for curing tobacco. 'Virginia' tobacco is flue-cured, the leaves being cured in barns by heat from furnaces for five to seven days. This preserves the sugar content of the tobacco. Burley, Maryland and cigar tobaccos are air-cured without heat for several weeks, during which time the sugars are digested. Oriental tobaccos are sun-cured with some loss of sugar. The tobacco in British cigarettes is almost all flue-cured.

Others are absorbed from the mouth, air passages, or air sacs in the lung into the blood and may then act on tissues throughout the body. The substances of medical importance in the smoke fall into four main groups—

a *Known cancer-producing substances*. These are of two kinds: carcinogens or cancer initiators, which have been shown by themselves to induce cancer in experimental animals, and co-carcinogens or cancer promoters, which do not themselves produce cancer but accelerate its production by cancer initiators.

b *Irritant substances*. These may stimulate secretion of mucus in the bronchial tubes and inhibit the action of the cilia* lining them. Some of these irritants are also co-carcinogens.

c *Nicotine*. This has a wide range of pharmacological actions on tissues throughout the body, especially on the nervous system.

d *Carbon monoxide and other gases*. Carbon monoxide interferes with the blood's capacity to carry oxygen or with the use of oxygen in the tissues. There are other chemically active gases, including oxides of nitrogen and hydrogen cyanide, the effects of which in the low concentrations occurring in tobacco smoke are uncertain.

Cancer Initiators and Promoters

3. 3   When tobacco smoke is condensed by cooling or by passage through a filter the particles in the smoke are collected as a dark brown, tarry material known as tobacco tar or tobacco condensate. This condensate, applied repeatedly and in sufficient quantity to the skin of mice or rabbits, gives rise to skin cancers [63a]. Earlier failures with such experiments were probably due to the use of insufficient material for too short a time. Cancer has also been produced by injections of condensate under the skin [54] or into the lungs of rats, or by painting it on to the trachea of dogs [53]. It has thus been

---

* Cilia are fine hair-like processes projecting into the bronchial tubes from the lining cells. By beating in a co-ordinated way they keep a film of mucus moving upward towards the throat. This is how inhaled dust and bacteria are continuously removed from healthy lungs.

established that tobacco smoke condensate contains substances that when applied to susceptible living tissues can cause cancer.

3. 4   In many experiments animals have been made to inhale cigarette smoke for various periods. The efficiency of the filtration by the noses of animals used is such that a large proportion of the smoke is removed before it reaches their lungs [63b]. Until recently there was only one report of an inhalation experiment with mice in which lung cancer had been induced and this was of a different type from human lung cancer [24]. Production of typical cancer of the larynx in hamsters by exposure to cigarette smoke has now been reported [20]. Furthermore, two out of twenty-four dogs taught to inhale cigarette smoke directly into the lungs by means of tubes inserted into their windpipes have now developed lung cancer, similar to the human disease, after two and a half years of smoking seven unfiltered cigarettes daily. Ten developed other types of lung cancer. Dogs which had smoked the same number of filtered cigarettes during the same period did not develop cancer though some showed precancerous changes [7].

3. 5   Many individual chemical compounds isolated from various forms of tobacco smoke condensate have been tested for carcinogenic activity, mainly on the skin of mice. The principal conclusions to be drawn are the following:

3. 6   *Cancer initiators.* The chief initiators of cancer are substances known as polycyclic aromatic hydrocarbons. Other substances in tobacco smoke that can initiate cancer [63c] occur in such small amounts that they are unlikely to make an important contribution to cancer production by tobacco smoke. One such substance is polonium 210, a radioactive element, present in main-stream smoke [38, 39, 40, 48, 49, 58e]. There is considerable controversy about the possible role of radioactivity in the production of cancer by cigarette smoke and no conclusion is at present possible [27, 49].

3. 7   *Cancer promoters.* Substances found in tobacco smoke that enhance the action of cancer initiators include phenols, fatty acid esters, and free fatty acids [63c]. Many of these are also irritants (para 3. 11).

3. 8 *Cancer-producing effects of condensates from different types of tobacco*. The cancer-producing action of tobacco smoke condensates in animals is affected by the type of tobacco, the way it is burnt, the filters used, the method of condensation, and the method of application to the test animal [63*a, d, e*]. Although smoking pipes or cigars is less liable than cigarette smoking to cause lung cancer in man (para. 4. 13), condensates from pipe or cigar smoke contain more polycyclic hydrocarbons [11] and are more carcinogenic to animal skin than condensates from the smoke of similar amounts of cigarette tobaccos [16, 29].

3. 9 *Reduction of cancer production by tobacco condensate*. Filtered cigarettes produce less condensate than similar plain cigarettes, so that the resultant condensate is, per cigarette smoked, less carcinogenic. Filters have been developed which selectively remove some cancer initiators or promoters from smoke [63*e*]. The amount of smoke condensate from some tobaccos is less than from others, and the condensates from different tobaccos may vary widely in their cancer-producing properties. The addition of certain chemicals [8], such as nitrates [28], which make the tobacco burn more rapidly, also reduces the amount of condensate and its carcinogenic action [28, 63*f*]. A similar effect results from treatment of the paper by, for instance, ammonium sulphamate, which brings about more efficient burning of tobacco [63*g*]. Little is known about the effects of such modified cigarettes in man, especially since the sort of exposure to which the smoker subjects himself cannot be reproduced exactly in animals.

3. 10 *Relevance of experimental studies to human lung cancer*. The direct evidence that cigarette smoking causes cancer of the lung in man, reviewed in Chapter 4, is so clear that no experiments are needed to confirm it. The results of animal experiments must always be applied with caution to man. Experiments have shown, for example, that the condensates from pipe and cigar smoke are more effective in producing cancer in animals than is cigarette smoke [16, 29]. Nevertheless in man, the risk of lung cancer is much greater for the cigarette smoker than for the smoker of pipes and cigars (para. 4. 13). Animal experiments could point to possible modifications of cigarettes that might make them less dangerous. Lung cancer in dogs provides a more relevant experimental method for testing the cancer risks of different kinds of cigarettes (para 3. 4), but the ultimate measure of risk can be derived only from prolonged study of the men and women who smoke them.

Irritant Substances in Tobacco Smoke [63c]

3. 11   These include substances responsible for the immediate coughing and narrowing of the bronchial tubes that follow inhalation of tobacco smoke, for arresting the beating of the cilia (ciliostatic effect), and for stimulating bronchial glands to secrete increased amounts of mucus. Not all of the substances have been identified.

3. 12   The ciliostatic effect of various components of tobacco smoke can be studied only in the laboratory. Ten or more compounds, of which acrolein seems to be one of the most important [60], are ciliostatic, an effect produced by both the particulate and vapour phases of the smoke [15]. This action may contribute to the causes of pulmonary disease by interfering with the self-cleansing mechanism of the lung [1], thus encouraging infection and allowing more prolonged contact between the lining of the bronchial tubes and the cancer-producing substances in the smoke.

3. 13   Both the vapour and particulate phases of the smoke are concerned in the immediate narrowing of the bronchi that occurs on smoking. The bronchial reaction is reduced by filters which remove either the particulate or vapour phases of the smoke [13]; it is not due to nicotine [44]. Cigar smoke, when inhaled, is in this respect more irritating than cigarette smoke [51] and at least as likely to bring on coughing, but it is not usually inhaled. Animals exposed to tobacco smoke develop pathological changes resembling those of chronic bronchitis and emphysema in man [6, 25, 34, 52]. There is little difference between the severity of bronchitic changes produced in rats by smoke from cigarette and cigar tobaccos, but those exposed to cigarette smoke have a higher mortality from lung infections than those exposed to cigar smoke, and have been found to develop changes in the bronchial tubes

that are more suggestive of the early stages of cancer [33, 34].

Nicotine and Nicotine Dependence

3. 14　The amount of nicotine recoverable from mainstream smoke of different brands of British cigarettes ranges from 0·4 to 3 mg per cigarette. Smokers who inhale may absorb as much as 90 per cent of this, and those who do not inhale as little as 10 per cent. Absorption of nicotine depends both on the type of tobacco and on the way it is smoked. The exact amount absorbed by a smoker is difficult to measure directly [17, 31], but it has been estimated that the average smoker who inhales absorbs with every puff a dose of nicotine which is equivalent to about 0·1 mg given intravenously [2]. Nicotine in alkaline smoke (as that from pipe or cigar tobaccos) is absorbed through the lining of the mouth and pharynx, but nicotine in the acid smoke of cigarettes is absorbed chiefly after it has been inhaled into the lungs. Thus, some nicotine from pipe and cigar smoke can be absorbed without inhaling, and it may be because of this and the greater irritant effect of pipe and cigar smoke that pipe and cigar smokers seldom inhale. Cigarette smokers inhale more and have been found to absorb about three times as much nicotine as cigar and pipe smokers because of this [31]. The main actions of nicotine are on the nervous system and, indirectly, on the heart and blood vessels, the blood, and the kidneys.

3. 15　*Action of nicotine on nerve cells.* In the brain, as elsewhere in the body, the transmission of nervous impulses from one cell to another is due to the release at nerve endings of chemicals called neurotransmitters; these include acetylcholine and noradrenaline. Nicotine can mimic this action, but since it first stimulates and later inhibits transmission of nerve impulses its effects are complex and variable.

3. 16　In animals it can be shown that nicotine is located in the brain in relatively high concentrations within a few minutes of intravenous injection [55]. In rats and cats this brings about the release of acetylcholine from the brain [3, 4]; the same thing happens when a sleeping cat wakes up [12]. This release of acetylcholine is accompanied by

alterations in the electrical activity of the brain indicating arousal [4]. Similar changes follow the introduction of cigarette smoke into the lungs of cats. There is, however, considerable variation between different animals, for in some of them nicotine lowers the activity of the brain [46]. In rats nicotine tends to increase the activity of inactive animals but may depress the activity of those which are more active [10, 41]. These effects are probably due to the release of acetylcholine in the brain. Nicotine may also make rats better able to learn how to negotiate a maze [22]. Since this result could also be produced by injecting nicotine after each daily learning procedure it has been suggested that it may facilitate the memory process, but the results of such experiments vary with the species and strain of animals used.

3. 17 The results of these experiments in animals are consistent with the claims of smokers that smoking may prevent drowsiness and facilitate study while having a sedative effect in stressful situations, and with the fact that some smokers emphasise the sedative but others the stimulant effects.

3. 18 There have been few direct experiments on these effects on the nervous system in man. Administration of small doses of nicotine or smoking produces changes in tests of brain activity [61] and the electroencephalogram [43] that indicate arousal. On the other hand, there is objective evidence for a tranquillising effect on the nervous system in that smoking a cigarette depresses the knee-jerk reflex; the depression is greater in non-smokers and light smokers than in heavy smokers [14].

3. 19 Nicotine from smoking certainly has important actions on the human central nervous system, which include stimulation and sedation depending on the dose, on how much is normally smoked, on the state of activity of the smoker and on his individual constitution and psychological make-up. Evidence that the difficulty that many smokers find in giving up the habit is due to habituation to nicotine is scanty. It has been reported on the basis of a few uncontrolled experiments that nicotine injections may reduce the desire for a cigarette and may themselves induce some dependence (para 8. 18). Tobacco manufacturers find in

consumer studies that the 'satisfaction' of a cigarette is reduced when the nicotine delivered falls below 1 mg per cigarette, and there is experimental evidence that some smokers given low nicotine cigarettes without realising it increase the number of puffs per cigarette to restore their previous intake of nicotine [64].

3. 20 *The actions of nicotine on the heart and blood vessels.* Cigarette smoking releases the hormones adrenaline and noradrenaline from the adrenal glands so that their concentration in the blood stream is greater than they otherwise would be; nicotine injection has the same effect [2, 36c]. The main actions of smoking on the heart and blood vessels are due to this. Nicotine from smoking and by injection also acts directly on the nervous centres that control blood pressure and heart rate [2]. In normal men smoking [30] or inhaling nicotine [26] causes an increase in heart rate, in output of blood by the heart, and in blood pressure, and constriction of the blood-vessels. In smokers with coronary heart disease, however, the heart's output of blood may fail to rise [21] or may fall [45] on smoking a cigarette, and there may be abnormal beats that could endanger anyone with a diseased heart [58c].

3. 21 Smoking or injecting nicotine tends to increase the concentration of fatty acids in the blood [58b] and also the liability of blood platelets to adhere to each other and to the walls of blood vessels [58c]. These actions are early stages in thrombosis (clotting) of the blood, and may be concerned in the formation of atheroma of the arteries (para 6. 1). This may be why the coronary arteries of cigarette smokers have more atherosclerosis than those of non-smokers (para 6. 7).

3. 22 *Other actions of nicotine.* Smoking or injection of nicotine releases a hormone from the pituitary gland (antidiuretic hormone) which temporarily reduces the output of urine [36a]. This hormone may also raise blood pressure. In animals nicotine raises the level of blood sugar, but these effects of smoking are variable in man [35, 36b].

Carbon Monoxide

3. 23 Carbon monoxide occurs in high concentration in

cigarette smoke: it is diluted by air on inhalation, and an estimate of the average concentration in smoke inhaled into the lung is about 400 parts per million. Since its affinity for haemoglobin, which carries oxygen in the blood, is much greater than that of oxygen, this results in the loss of up to 10 per cent of the capacity of the blood of smokers to transport oxygen [23]. Heart muscle has a great demand for oxygen, and if coronary artery disease has interfered with its blood supply it could be additionally handicapped by carbon monoxide. It is also possible that in such cases the heart function is impaired not only by reduction of the oxygen carried to it but also by impairment of the efficiency with which it uses the oxygen it receives, which could result from the action of cyanates (derived from hydrogen cyanide in tobacco smoke) on its metabolism. All these effects could endanger life after coronary thrombosis. Cigarette smokers have more carbon monoxide in their blood than pipe and cigar smokers [50]. Exposure to carbon monoxide has been shown to increase atheroma formation in experimental animals and a similar effect in man may be one of the reasons for the increased risk that smokers have of developing diseases of the heart and blood vessels [5, 32] (Chapter 6).

3. 24　This impairment of the efficiency of oxygen transport and use is unimportant in healthy young adults in their ordinary activities but could be one factor in limiting the athletic performance of smokers (para 7. 26). It may also interfere with the growth of the unborn child (para 7. 2).

REFERENCES

1. ALBERT, R.E., LIPPMANN, M., and BRISCOE, W. (1969). 'The characteristics of bronchial clearance in humans and the effects of cigarette smoking.' *Archs. envir. Hlth*, **18**, 738.

2. ARMITAGE, A. K. (1965). 'Effects of nicotine and tobacco smoke on blood pressure and release of catecholamines from the adrenal glands.' *Br. J. Pharmac.*, **25**, 515.

3. ARMITAGE, A. K., HALL, G. H., and MORRISON, C. F. (1968). 'Pharmacological basis for the tobacco smoking habit.' *Nature Lond.*, **217**, 331.

4. ARMITAGE, A. K., HALL, G. M., and SELLERS, C. M. (1969). 'Effects of nicotine on electrocortical activity and acetylcholine release from the cat cerebral cortex.' *Br. J. Pharmac.*, **35**, 152.

5. Astrup, P., Kjeldsen, K., and Wanstrup, J. (1967). 'Enhancing influence of carbon monoxide on the development of atheromatosis in cholesterol-fed rabbits.' *J. Atheroscler. Res.*, **7**, 343.

6. Auerbach, O., Hammond, E. C., Kirman, D., Garfinkel, L., and Stout, A. P. (1967). 'Histologic changes in bronchial tubes of cigarette smoking dogs.' *Cancer, N.Y.*, **20**, 2055.

7. Auerbach, O., and Hammond, E. C. (1970). 'Smoking gives dogs invasive lung cancer.' *Med. News Tribune*, Feb. 27, p. 3.

8. Bentley, H. R., and Burgan, J. G. (1960). 'Polynuclear hydrocarbons in tobacco and tobacco smoke.' *Analyst, Lond.*, **85**, 723.

9. Blacklock, J. W. S. (1961). 'An experimental study of the pathological effects of cigarette condensate in the lungs with special reference to carcinogenesis.' *Br. J. Cancer*, **15**, 745.

10. Bovet, D., Bovet-Nitti, F., and Oliverio, A. (1967). 'Action of nicotine on spontaneous and acquired behaviour of rats and mice.' *Ann. N.Y. Acad. Sci.*, **142**, 261.

11. Campbell, J. M., and Lindsey, A. J. (1957). 'Polycylic hydrocarbons in cigar smoke.' *Br. J. Cancer*, **11**, 192.

12. Celesia, C. G., and Jasper, H. H. (1966). 'Acetylcholine released from cerebral cortex in relation to state of activation.' *Neurology, Minneap.*, **16**, 1053.

13. Clarke, B. G., Guyatt, A. R., Alpers, J. H., Fletcher, C. M., and Hill, I. D. (1970). 'Changes in airways conductance on smoking a cigarette. A study of repeatability and of the effect of particulate and vapour phase filters.' *Thorax*, **25**, 418.

14. Clark, M. S. G., and Rand, M. J. (1968). 'Effect of tobacco smoke on the knee-jerk reflex in man.' *Europ. J. Pharmacol.*, **3**, 294,

15. Dalhamn, T. (1966). 'Effect of cigarette smoke on ciliary activity.' *Am. Rev. resp. Dis.*, **93**, (March) Suppl., 108.

16. Davies, R. F., and Day, T. D. (1969). 'A study of the comparative carcinogenicity of cigarette and cigar smoke condensate on mouse skin.' *Br. J. Cancer*, **23**, 363.

17. Desoille, H., Truffert, L., Lebbe, J., Cremer, G., and Girard-Wallon. (1963). 'Dépistage des fumeurs par le dosage de la nicotine dans le sang.' *Archs. Mal. prof. Méd. trav.*, **24**, 422.

18. Dobrowsky, A. (1964). 'Verrauchung und Redistillation in Theorie und Versuchen.' *Beitr. Tabakforsch.*, **2**, 237.

19. Domino, E. F., and Von Baumgarten, A. M. (1969). 'Tobacco cigarette smoking and patellar reflex depression.' *Clin. Pharmac. Ther.*, **10**, 72.

20. Dontenwill, W. (1970). Laryngeal cancer in hamsters exposed to cigarette smoke. (In press.)

21. Frankl, W. S., Winters, W. L., and Soloff, L. A. (1965). 'The effects of smoking on the cardiac output at rest and during exercise in patients with healed myocardial infarction.' *Circulation*, **31**, 42.

22. Garg, M., and Holland, H. C. (1968). 'Consolidation and maze learning. A further study of post-trial injection of a stimulant drug (nicotine).' *Int. J. Neuropharmacol.*, **7**, 55.

23. Goldsmith, J. R., and Landaw, S. A. (1968). 'Carbon monoxide and human health.' *Science N.Y.*, **162**, 1352.

24. HARRIS, R. J. C., and NEGRONI, G. (1967). 'Production of lung carcinomas in C57BL mice exposed to a cigarette smoke and air mixture.' *Br. med. J.*, **4**, 637.

25. HERNANDEZ, J. A., ANDERSON, A. E., HOLMES, W. L., and FORAKER, A. G. (1966). 'Pulmonary parenchymal defects in dogs following prolonged cigarette smoke exposure.' *Am. Rev. resp. Dis.*, **93**, 78.

26. HERXHEIMER, A., GRIFFITHS, R. L., HAMILTON, B., and WAKEFIELD, M. (1967). 'Circulatory effects of nicotine aerosol inhalation and cigarette smoking in man.' *Lancet*, **2**, 754.

27. HILL, C. R. (1964). 'Polonium-210 in man.' *Nature, Lond.*, **208**, 423.

28. HOFFMANN, D., and WYNDER, E. L. (1967). 'The reduction of the tumorigenicity of cigarette smoke condensate by addition of sodium nitrate to tobacco.' *Cancer Res.*, **27**, 172.

29. HOMBURGER, F., TREGER, A., and BAKER, J. R. (1963). 'Mouse skin painting with smoke condensate from cigarettes made of pipe, cigar and cigarette tobaccos.' *J. natn. Cancer Inst.*, **31**, 1445.

30. KERRIGAN, R., JAIN, A. C., and DOYLE, J. T. (1968). 'The circulatory response to cigarette smoking at rest and after exercise.' *Am. J. med. Sci.*, **255**, 113.

31. KERSHBAUM, A., BELLET, S., HIRABAYASHI, M., FEINBERG, L. J., and EILBERG, R. (1967). 'Effect of cigarette, cigar and pipe smoking on nicotine excretion. The influence of inhaling.' *Archs. intern. Med.* **120**, 311.

32. KJELDSEN, K. (1949). *Smoking and Atherosclerosis*. Munksgaard, Copenhagen.

33. LAMB, D. (1967). 'Histological changes in the tracheobronchial epithelium of rats exposed to tobacco smoke' (abstract) *Thorax*, **22**, 290.

34. LAMB, D., and REID, L. (1969). 'Goblet cell increase in rat bronchial epithelium after exposure to cigarette and cigar tobacco smoke.' *Br. med. J.*, **1**, 33.

35. LARSON, P. S., HAAG, H. B., and SILVETTE, H. (1961). *Tobacco: experimental and clinical Studies. A comprehensive account of the world literature*. Williams and Wilkins Co., Baltimore, p. 325.

36. LARSON, P. S., and SILVETTE, H. (1968). *Tobacco: experimental and clinical Studies. A Comprehensive account of the world literature*. Supplement. Williams and Wilkins Co., Baltimore, *a*, p. 153; *b*, p. 173; *c*, pp. 194–8.

37. LINDSEY, A. (1959). 'The composition of cigarette smoke. Studies on stubs and tips.' *Br. J. Cancer*, **13**, 195.

38. LITTLE, J. B., RADFORD, E. P., McCOMBS, H. L., and HUNT, V. R. (1965). Distribution of polonium-210 in pulmonary tissue of cigarette smokers.' *New Engl. J. Med.*, **273**, 1343.

39. MARSDEN, E. (1964). 'Incidence and possible significance of inhaled or ingested polonium.' *Nature, Lond.*, **203**, 230.

40. MARSDEN, E. (1965). 'Some aspects of the relationship of radioactivity to lung cancer.' *N.Z. med. J.*, **64**, 367.

41. MORRISON, C. F., and LEE, P. N. (1968). 'A comparison of the effects of nicotine and physostigmine on a measure of activity in the rat.' *Psychopharmacologia* **13**, 210.

42. MULLER, K. H., NEURATH, G., and HORSTMANN, H. (1964). 'Einfluss der luftdurchschlässigkeit von cigaretten papier auf die ausbeute und zusammensetzung des rauches.' *Beitr. Tabakforsch.*, **2**, 271.

43. MURPHREE, H. B., PFEIFFER, C. C., and PRICE, L. M. (1967). 'Electroencephalographic changes in man following smoking.' *Ann. N.Y. Acad. Sci.*, **142**, 245.

44. NADEL, J. A., and COMROE, J. H. (1961). 'Acute effects of inhalation of cigarette smoke on airway conductance.' *J. appl. Physiol.*, **16**, 713.

45. PENTECOST, B., and SHILLINGFORD, J. (1964). 'The acute effects of smoking on myocardial performance in patients with coronary arterial disease.' *Br. Heart J.*, **26**, 422.

46. PHILLIS, J. W., and YORK, D. H. (1968). 'Nicotine, smoking and cortical inhibition.' *Nature, Lond.*, **219**, 89.

47. PROVOST, A. (1959). *Technique du Tabac*. Heliographia, Lausanne, pp. 35–6.

48. RADFORD, E. P., and HUNT, V. R. (1964). 'Cigarettes and polonium-210. *Science, N.Y.*, **144**, 366.

49. RADFORD, E. P., HUNT, V. R., and LITTLE, J. B. (1969). 'Carcinogenicity of tobacco smoke constituents.' *Science, N.Y.*, **165**, 312.

50. RINGOLD, A., GOLDSMITH, J. R., HELWIG, H. L., FINN, R., and SCHUETTE, F. (1962). 'Estimating recent carbon monoxide exposure. A rapid method.' *Archs. envir. Hlth.*, **5**, 308.

51. ROBERTSON, D. G., WARRELL, D. A., NEWTON-HOWES, J. S., and FLETCHER, C. M. (1969). 'Bronchial reactivity to cigarette and cigar smoke.' *Br. med. J.*, **3**, 269.

52. ROCKEY, E. E., and SPEER, F. D. (1966). 'The ill effects of cigarette smoking in dogs.' *Int. Surg.*, **46**, 520.

53. ROCKEY, E. E., SPEER, F. D., AHN, K. J., THOMPSON, S. A., and HIROSE, I. (1962). 'The effect of cigarette smoke condensate on the bronchial mucosa of dogs.' *Cancer, N.Y.*, **15**, 1100.

54. SCHMAHL, D., and THOMAS, C. (1964). 'Vergleichende Prüfung von Tabakrauchkondensaten bei subcutaner und oralet Applikation auf cancerogene Wirkung bei Ratten.' *Z. Krebsforsch*, **66**, 291.

55. SCHMITERLÖW, C. G., HANSON, E., ANDERSSON, G., APPELGREN, L. E., and HOFFMANN, P. C. (1967). 'Distribution of nicotine in the central nervous system.' *Ann. N.Y. Acad. Sci.*, **142**, 2.

56. SEGELKEN, D., SCHRÖDER, R., and SEEHOFER, F. (1962). 'Die Rauchkondensatemenge von Zigaretten in Abhangigkeit von der Zugzahl bzw. Zugnummer. *Tabak. Tech. Hamburg Tech. Wiss. Schr. No.* 31. Quoted Wynder & Hoffmann 1967. p. 509.

57. US PUBLIC HEALTH SERVICE (1967). *Health Consequences of Smoking.* Public Health Service publication No. 1696, pp. 64, 30, 81.

58. US PUBLIC HEALTH SERVICE (1968). Supplement to Public Health Service Publication No. 1696. *a*, p. 30; *b*, p. 32; *c*, p. 34; *d*, p. 38; *e*, p. 92.

59. US PUBLIC HEALTH SERVICE (1969). Supplement to Public Health Service Publication No. 1696. *a*, p. 27; *b*, p. 28.

60. WALKER, T. R., and KIEFER, J. E. (1966). 'Ciliastatic components in the gas phase of cigarette smoke.' *Science, N.Y.*, **153**, 1248.

61. WARWICK, K. M., and EYSENCK, H. J. (1968). 'Experimental studies of the behavioural effects of nicotine.' *Pharmakopsychiatrie Neuro-psychopharmakologie*, **1**, 145.

62. WOLF, F. A. (1967). *Tobacco Production and Processing*. Reference 63, p. 5.

63. WYNDER, E. L., and HOFFMANN, D. (1967). *Tobacco and Tobacco Smoke. Studies in experimental carcinogenesis*. Academic Press, New York and London. *a*, p. 181; *b*, p. 202; *c*, pp. 496–501; *d*, p. 516; *e*, p. 519; *f*, p. 521; *g*, p. 529.

64. ASHTON, H., and WATSON, D. W. (1970). 'Puffing frequency and nicotine intake in cigarette smokers.' *Br. med. J.*, **3**, 679.

4 Smoking and Cancer of the Lung

4. 1   During recent years the world-wide increase in numbers of deaths from lung cancer has continued almost unabated [58, 59, 67]. Men are affected more than women everywhere. The recent trends of mortality from lung cancer in British men between the ages of 45 and 64, when family and professional responsibilities are at their height, are shown in Figure 4. 1. Since 1966, death rates have been declining slightly in men at these ages but increasing in women. This recent small decline in death rates among men aged 45 to 64 may be associated with the reduction in cigarette smoking some twenty years earlier from the extremely high level during the second world war (Figure 1. 1). In 1968 in the United Kingdom some 27,000 men and 5,500 women died from lung cancer. About one half of these deaths occurred before the age of 65. The proportion of all deaths due to lung cancer was greatest in men at the age of 55 to 64, when it was one in every seven deaths, and in women at the age of 45 to 54 when it was one in every twenty deaths. (Table 4. 1).

4. 2   Many countries have set up authoritative committees and commissions to study the cause of this modern scourge [19, 52, 53, 56, 57, 64, 70, 76, 83]. All have concluded that it is almost entirely due to cigarette smoking. A small number of individuals [6, 12, 28, 29, 34, 38, 39a, 40, 50, 84] have challenged these expert conclusions, and some have publicised their criticisms. This may explain why nearly nine out of every ten smokers in this country believe that 'experts disagree' about this question, and that cigarette smoking has not yet been proved to be the main cause of lung cancer [51]. It is therefore necessary to recapitulate the facts on which the conclusion that cigarette smoking causes this disease is based,

to discuss and answer objections to this conclusion, and to consider the future trends of lung cancer deaths that are to be expected in Britain if no effective preventive action is taken.

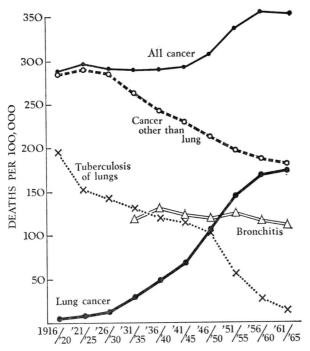

Figure 4. 1 *Death rates from lung cancer, other forms of cancer, tuberculosis of the lung, and bronchitis in men aged 45–64 from 1916–1965.* In England and Wales the increasing death rate from lung cancer is striking. The decline in deaths from other forms of cancer has occurred chiefly in respect of cancer of the liver, tongue, oesophagus, and rectum. At first the rise in lung cancer cancelled out this decline so that the total death rate from all cancers was constant, but in the last 25 years the overall death rate from cancer has risen largely because of the rising lung cancer rate. The sharper decline of tuberculous mortality in the last twenty years is due to modern antibiotics. Because of changes in the practice of death registration before 1931 the earlier figures for bronchitis are not comparable to subsequent ones and have been omitted. Since 1931, they have changed very little in middle-aged men.

TABLE 4. 1

Number and percentage of deaths from chief diseases related to smoking in men and women aged 35 and over: United Kingdom 1968

Age	Lung cancer		Chronic Bronchitis		Coronary heart disease		All causes	
	Number	%	*Number*	%	*Number*	%	*Number*	%
I MEN								
35–44	516	6·3	160	1·9	2,162	26·3	8,220	100
45–54	2,910	11·9	1,095	4·5	8,183	33·4	24,481	100
55–64	9,068	13·7	5,237	7·9	20,668	31·1	66,381	100
35–64	**12,494**	**12·6**	**6,492**	**6·6**	**31,013**	**31·3**	**99,082**	**100**
65–74	10,310	10·4	9,734	9·8	27,902	28·2	98,937	100
75 and over	4,169	3·6	8,750	7·6	26,977	23·6	114,518	100
35 and over	**26,973**	**8·6**	**24,976**	**8·0**	**85,892**	**2·75**	**312,537**	**100**
II WOMEN								
35–44	179	3·1	82	1·4	336	5·8	5,744	100
45–54	791	5·3	385	2·6	1,319	8·8	14,933	100
55–64	1,573	4·3	1,042	2·8	5,927	16·1	36,806	100
35–64	**2,543**	**4·4**	**1,509**	**2·6**	**7,582**	**13·2**	**57,483**	**100**
65–74	1,865	2·5	2,269	3·0	16,326	21·8	74,936	100
75 and over	1,157	0·7	4,159	2·4	27,945	15·9	175,629	100
35 and over	**5,565**	**1·8**	**7,937**	**2·6**	**51,853**	**16·8**	**308,048**	**100**

From extracts of Table 17 from Part I of the Registrar General's Statistical Review of England and Wales for the year 1968, Table C2.1 from Part I of the Annual Report of the Registrar General for Scotland, 1968, and Abstract 12 from the Forty Seventh Annual Report of the Registrar General for Northern Ireland, 1968. Lung Cancer: ICD Nos. 162.1, 163.0; Chronic Bronchitis: ICD Nos. 491, 492; Coronary Heart Disease: ICD Nos. 410.9, 411.9, 412.9, 413.9, 414.9 (only Scotland publishes coronary heart disease statistics in this form, statistics for England and Wales and Northern Ireland have been estimated from ICD Nos. 410–414 on the basis of the Scottish experience).

Evidence from Human Experience

4. 3 *Retrospective studies.* More than thirty investigations in ten countries [21, 42, 47a, 76a] have shown that when the previous smoking habits of patients with lung cancer are analysed there are many more heavy smokers and fewer light smokers and non-smokers than among patients of the same sex and age and place of residence without lung cancer. These studies have consistently demonstrated a direct association between the number of cigarettes smoked and the incidence of the disease.*

4. 4 *Prospective studies.* In these investigations the smoking habits of large numbers of people are recorded during life, and when they die the causes of death are ascertained [7, 26a, 36, 37, 43, 47b, 76b]. This method obviates some of the sources of bias encountered in retrospective studies, which record smoking habits after the patient has developed the disease [76c]. Eight such prospective studies are in close agreement in disclosing a steady rise in lung cancer with increasing numbers of cigarettes smoked. Figure 4. 2 shows the results of four of these, giving information about nearly 1,430,000 persons investigated for periods ranging from four to more than ten years.

4. 5 The evidence thus established, that the risk of lung cancer grows in direct relation to the numbers of cigarettes smoked, has been criticised on various grounds [6, 12, 28, 29, 30]. For example, in none of the studies are the subjects a random and fully representative sample of the general population nor has the response to the enquiry been as large as is usually demanded in this sort of survey. The doctors in the British investigation, for instance, are a group selected by occupation, and only 66 per cent of those invited to take part agreed to do so. The death rates in those who did not respond were higher than in those who did. In both this and in the American work the mortality rate from lung cancer was lower than in the general population. The measurements of mortality thus made cannot be exactly applied to any

---

* There are only two discordant studies—one of postmortem material [60] and the other of employees in the tobacco industry [17]—both of which have been shown to have been statistically unsound [45, 72c].

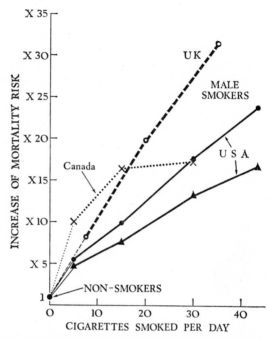

Figure 4. 2 *Relationship between numbers of cigarettes smoked per day and lung cancer death rates from four prospective studies (males only).* The figure shows how much the risk of dying from lung cancer is multiplied in those who smoke various numbers of cigarettes per day compared with the risk of non-smokers. Thus, X 30 indicates that the risk is 30 times as great as in non-smokers. The figures are derived from Doll and Hill's study of British doctors aged 35 years and over [26a]; Hammond's study of American men aged 40–79 [36]; Dorn's study of American ex-service men aged 30 and over [43]; and Best's study of Canadian veterans [7].

The steady rise in lung-cancer risk with increasing cigarette smoking found by the British and the two American studies is impressive. It is not clear why the heavier smokers showed a less striking increase in the Canadian study. The higher British rate may be due to the British habit of smoking cigarettes to a shorter stub length than the Americans and to the greater exposure of British men to air polluted by domestic and industrial smoke [27, 35].

population as a whole. Nevertheless it is impossible to deny that cigarette smokers run an increased risk of lung cancer and that this is closely related to the number of cigarettes smoked.

4. 6   Another criticism relates to the numbers of cigarettes smoked. The figures were obtained at the beginning of the survey and may be only rough indications of life-time smoking habits. Moreover, smokers vary in the way they smoke: in the depth of inhalation, the length of cigarette smoked, the rate of smoking, the number of puffs taken, the length of time the cigarette is held in the mouth, the age at which the habit began, and the types of cigarette. When these factors have been looked into separately, they have not been found to alter materially the conclusions based on simple estimates of the numbers of cigarettes smoked daily, but confirm that the greater the exposure to cigarette smoke the greater the risk of developing lung cancer.

The Influence of Variations in Smoking Habits

4. 7   *Inhalation.* Heavy smokers inhale most, and younger smokers inhale more than their elders [73]. The death rate from lung cancer in the British doctors who said they inhaled was 80 per cent greater than those who said they did not [26a]. American workers observed similar differences between inhalers and non-inhalers [36, 76d]; and a much higher death rate from this disease in non-inhalers than in non-smokers.

4. 8   *Age of starting to smoke.* In the largest American study [36], men who had begun smoking before the age of 15 had a death rate from lung cancer five times higher than those who had begun after the age of 25. Those who had started at intermediate ages had intermediate risks.

4. 9   *Other variations in manner of smoking cigarettes.* The hazard of lung cancer is increased in those who take more puffs per cigarette than others, especially towards the end, by the time taken to smoke it [33], by keeping it in the mouth between puffs [9], and by re-lighting half-smoked cigarettes [20].

4. 10   *Filter-tipped cigarettes.* Filter tips that may reduce the

amount of 'tar' the smoker takes into his lungs have not been in general use in Britain long enough to determine their effect on liability to lung cancer. One American retrospective survey [11] has, however, suggested that men who had switched to smoking only filtered cigarettes during the previous ten years incurred a risk of contracting the disease that was significantly lower (by some 40 per cent) than that of men who had not switched. A recent experiment in the production of lung tumours in dogs has demonstrated the protective effect of filters (para 3. 4).

4. 11   *Reduced risk in those who stop smoking.* Those who give up smoking cigarettes are much less likely to get cancer of the lung than those who continue; the excess risk decreases rapidly after stopping. In British doctors [26a] who had stopped smoking the risk fell within five years to about one half of that of continuing smokers and after fifteen years was only three times the very small risk of non-smokers (Figure 4. 3).

4. 12   Between 1951 and 1965 half of all the doctors included in this study who used to smoke cigarettes stopped smoking (para 1. 5). Over this period, while lung cancer death rates among all men aged 35 to 64 in England and Wales rose by 7 per cent they fell by 38 per cent among male doctors of the same age [26b] (Figure 4. 4). This finding not only confirms that cigarette smoking causes lung cancer but also indicates that general discontinuance of the habit would lower the number of deaths from this disease.

4. 13   *Pipe and cigar smokers.* British, American, and Canadian workers found that the chance of getting lung cancer was less for men who had smoked only pipes than for those who had also smoked cigarettes: these mixed smokers had a risk similar to that of those smoking the same number of cigarettes only [26a, 36, 43]. In America there were enough cigar smokers for their liability to be measured separately; the risk was only twice as large as in abstainers (Figure 4. 5). But in Swiss and German retrospective surveys [1, 62], the risk of lung cancer appeared to be greater among pipe and cigar smokers than among cigarette smokers. Hitherto, the numbers who have changed from cigarettes to pipes or cigars have been too small

to show any effect on cancer of the lung. Possible explanations for the difference between pipe or cigar smokers and cigarette smokers are considered in para 4. 23.

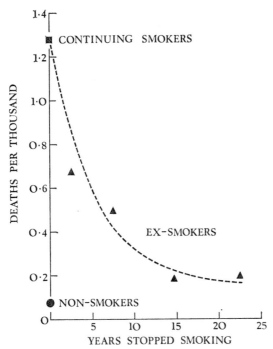

Figure 4. 3 *Standardised death rates from lung cancer for cigarette smokers and ex-smokers for various periods and for non-smokers.* This figure is derived from Doll and Hill's study of British doctors [26a] and is based on smoking habits of doctors at the beginning of the ten-year follow-up. Continuing smokers were those who were smoking cigarettes at the beginning of the study and the ex-smokers have been classified according to the number of years that they had stopped smoking before the study began. Non-smokers were those who had never regularly smoked cigarettes at the beginning of the study. Continuing smokers have a greatly increased risk of lung cancer but this risk is halved in those who had stopped between one and five years, and in those who had stopped fifteen years is down to about twice that of non-smokers. Many cigarette smokers think that when they have smoked for twenty or more years it does not matter if they continue because they have already damaged their lungs. This figure shows the error of this view.

Structural Changes in the Lung

4. 14 Cilia normally keep a surface layer of mucus moving steadily towards the throat (para. 3. 2). Examination of the lungs of men and women dying from various conditions has shown that in cigarette smokers the ciliated cells are often replaced by flattened cells without cilia [2, 15, 41, 55, 66]. The deeper cells increase in number and many of them show changes which many pathologists regard as pre-cancerous; the greater the number of years of cigarette smoking the greater the frequency and extent of such changes. In people who have died with cancer of the lung these abnormalities

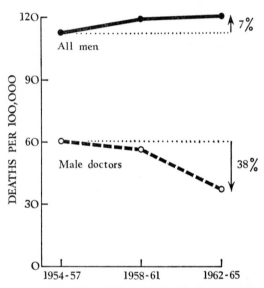

Figure 4. 4 *Death rates from lung cancer in male doctors and in all men in England and Wales.* These figures are derived from the Registrar General's Mortality returns and from Doll and Hill's study of British doctors [26*b*]. The rates for the two groups of men have been standardised for age. During the last twenty years many doctors have stopped smoking and their death rate from lung cancer has declined by 38 per cent while in all men in England and Wales who have not changed their cigarette consumption the rate has increased by 7 per cent. This experiment which doctors have carried out on themselves is strong evidence of the benefits that would result if there was widespread discontinuance of smoking.

are even more extensive, and there may be other smaller cancers in addition to the main growth that proved fatal [4]. In non-smokers and ex-smokers these changes are infrequent. Their rarity in ex-smokers [3] is consistent with the reduction in the risk of cancer when smokers give up the habit.

4. 15   There are three main forms of lung cancer: 'squamous' (in which the cells resemble those of the skin), 'small round celled' or 'oat-celled', and 'adenocarcinoma' (with a glandular structure). Only the first two much commoner types are related to cigarette smoking.

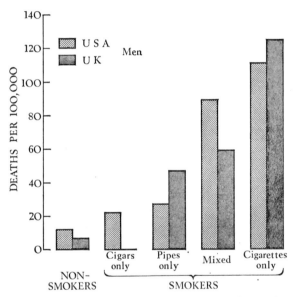

Figure 4. 5   *Death rates from lung cancer in men according to the type of tobacco smoked.* These figures are taken from the prospective study of British doctors aged 35 and over by Doll and Hill [26a] and the American study of men aged 40–79 by Hammond [36]. Only in the American study were there enough men who smoked only cigars to estimate their death rate, which was only twice that of non-smokers. Pipe smokers had two or three times the risk of non-smokers. Smokers of cigarettes together with pipe and cigar smokers (who smoke relatively few cigarettes) had six to eight times the risk, and smokers of cigarettes only between eleven times (USA) and twenty times (UK) the risk of non-smokers.

Other Environmental Causes of Lung Cancer

4. 16   Over 80 per cent of smokers in Britain consider that fog and fumes are more important causes of lung cancer than is smoking [51]. Analysis of the evidence brings out the error of this belief [65]. While the disease is commoner in urban than in rural areas, the difference cannot be attributed simply to different levels in air pollution. Concentrations of smoke in many of our cities have been falling steadily while the incidence of lung cancer has been rising. Men are only slightly more exposed to general air pollution than are women, but the disease is much commoner in men. Fumes from diesel engines, which have not escaped blame [54], cannot be responsible, because diesel fuels were widely used only after deaths from lung cancer had begun to rise. There also is little excess of the disease in persons specially exposed to motor exhausts [65]. Air pollution, particularly by coal smoke, appears to heighten the risk of lung cancer, but its effect is small compared with the effect of cigarette smoking. Men in certain occupations [23, 39], in particular those who have been exposed to asbestos dust [32, 68], chromates [8], nickel [22], arsenic [48], radioactive materials [79], mustard gas [78], and the products of coal distillation in the gas industry [25], have an increased liability to develop cancer of the lung. But the numbers who work in these occupations are too small to have much effect on the total number of deaths. In contrast to the former controversy about the effects of cigarette smoking, no one has doubted that these substances can cause lung cancer. Indeed, the evidence shows that the disease develops in response to inhalation of a variety of chemical agents of which cigarette smoke is simply the one to which more people are exposed than to any other.

Lung Cancer and Chronic Bronchitis

4. 17   Although cigarette smoking is an important cause of chronic bronchitis there has, in contrast to lung cancer, been no rise in deaths from this disease in recent years. This may be due in part to better treatment and also to less pollution of the air (para 5. 10). Several reports have suggested that smokers with a cough—or other evidence of chronic bronchitis —are more likely to develop cancer of the lung than those with no symptoms of bronchitis [10, 13, 14, 42, 63, 77, 82]. Unfortunately the significance of the difference is uncertain, and it offers no reassurance to cigarette smokers without a cough.

Experimental Evidence

4. 18   Many laboratory experiments have established that tobacco smoke condensate produces cancer of the skin in animals, and recent experiments showing that animals may also develop cancer of the larynx and lung from inhaling cigarette smoke (para 3. 4) have confirmed the observations already made in man.

Interpretation of the Evidence

4. 19   There has been a real, large, and world-wide rise in deaths from lung cancer during the past fifty years, and there is a close quantitative relationship between death rates from this disease and cigarette smoking. But some discrepancies must be discussed before it can be concluded that this relationship is one of cause and effect.

4. 20   *Differences between men and women.* In Britain, deaths from lung cancer are five times as frequent in men as in women whereas the present average cigarette consumption of men in Britain is only about twice as great. In both Doll and Hill's survey of British doctors [26a] and in Hammond's [36] in America, the death rate from lung cancer in women was found to be higher in heavier than in lighter cigarette smokers, but the women had lower rates than men who smoked similar amounts. There were enough female deaths in the American investigation to show that, as in men, the rate was higher in those who inhaled and in those who began smoking early in life.

4. 21   The question is whether women are less liable to lung cancer than men or whether there is any other explanation for these facts. Women's smoking habits differ from those of men in many important ways. In Britain, older women have on average begun later and inhale less [26a, 73]. In America it has been found that women, compared with men, do not

smoke cigarettes so far to the end, where the nicotine and 'tar' are concentrated during smoking. More of them smoke filter-tipped cigarettes and those with a low nicotine and 'tar' content. They also inhale less frequently and less deeply [80]. At older ages, when lung cancer is most common, not so many women smoke as men.

4. 22   It has been calculated that the life-time cigarette consumption of men aged 47 in 1964 was three times larger than that of women of the same age, while the male mortality from lung cancer between the ages of 45 and 49 was four times greater than the female rate [81]. If women continue to smoke more, to begin at an earlier age, and to smoke in the way men do, their death rate from this disease is likely to become nearly the same. It is to be noted that during the past two decades cigarette smoking has been increasing much more rapidly in women than in men, and the death rate from lung cancer in women has also been rising more rapidly (Figure 4. 6).

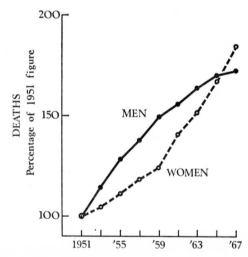

Figure 4. 6   *Standardised increases in lung cancer death rates for men and women 1951–1967.* During this period, cigarette smoking by women has increased steadily while in men it has decreased slightly. At present fewer women develop lung cancer but the rate of increase of the disease among them is faster than among men.

4. 23 *Lung cancer in pipe and cigar smokers.* It is not easy to account for the relatively low risk of lung cancer in pipe and cigar smokers since the amount of cancer-producing substances is, if anything, greater in pipe and cigar smoke than in smoke from cigarettes (para 3.8). The fact that pipe and cigar smoke is seldom inhaled may account for some of the difference, but the lung cancer rate in pipe and cigar smokers is lower than in cigarette smokers who deny inhalation [36]. Less serious changes in the lining of the bronchial tubes of rats exposed to smoke from cigarettes made from cigar tobacco than in those exposed to the smoke of ordinary cigarettes [46] suggest differences in the effects of these two kinds of smoke. Further study is needed on this.

Criticisms of and Alternatives to the Causal Hypothesis

4. 24 (*a*) *The evidence is 'only statistical.'* This objection cannot be sustained. Much of the evidence on the cause, prevention, and treatment of human disease is based on statistics; that is, on analysis of routinely or specially collected records of illnesses or deaths. The objection really implies that there is no experimental evidence from the laboratory to support the conclusion that cigarette smoking is responsible for lung cancer, but this is no longer true (para 3. 4). And it is possible to observe what is, in effect, an experiment in which millions of people who have been smoking cigarettes often develop lung cancer while millions of others who have abstained seldom do so. The only scientific loophole in the interpretation of these statistics is that the groups are self-selected. Since a controlled experiment in man is not feasible, the question of whether or not cigarette smoking causes cancer of the lung has to be judged on the evidence that is available.

4. 25 (*b*) *The 'non-specificity' of the association.* Two critics [6, 12] of the causal relation between cigarette smoking and lung cancer base their objections on the large number of diseases for which there are increased death rates for smokers. They appear to consider a unique 'one-to-one' relationship between cause and effect as fundamental to the concept of causation. There are two answers to this criticism. The first is advanced in a review from the US Department of Health, Education and Welfare [18], which points out that there is 'nothing contradictory nor inconsistent in the suggestion that one agent can be responsible for more than one disease . . . the great fog of London in 1952 increased the death rate for a number of causes, particularly respiratory and coronary disease but no-one has given this as a reason for doubting the causal role of the fog. . . . A universe in which cause and effect always had a one-to-one correspondence with each other would be easier to understand but it obviously is not the kind we inhabit.' The second is that cigarette smoke is not a single chemical agent (Chapter 3). It is unreasonable to expect that exposure over many years to so many potentially harmful components would increase liability to one disease only.

4. 26 (c) *The 'genetic' or 'constitutional' hypothesis.* If the causal explanation of the relation between cigarette smoking and lung cancer is to be rejected, an alternative hypothesis is required. The only serious alternative, advanced by a few statisticians [6, 12, 29] and a psychologist [28], is that people with an inherited liability to lung cancer also inherit a desire to smoke cigarettes and that the liability and desire are quantitatively related. In support of this hypothesis there is clear evidence from twin studies of a genetic or constitutional factor in smoking habits [29, 31, 61, 74]. Cigarette smokers have been shown to differ from non-smokers in their physical [69, 72] and psychological characteristics (para 8. 12). There is, however, little evidence of any inherited tendency to lung cancer. Small numbers of twin studies have hitherto provided no such evidence [16], but an increased tendency within family groups has been reported [75]. According to the genetic hypothesis the inborn liability, and hence the incidence of lung cancer, would be unaffected by persuading people to resist their inborn desire and stop smoking. But this is not so, as is shown by the experience of British doctors (Figures 4. 3 and 4. 4). As a group, their mortality from the disease has declined along with increasing abstention from cigarette smoking (para 4. 12), an abstention which is due not to any changed inborn desire but in large measure

to acceptance of the evidence that the habit is injurious to health.

4. 27   The chief reason for rejecting the genetic hypothesis is its inability to account for the enormous rise in death rates from lung cancer in the past half century. Proponents of the hypothesis have attempted to evade this objection on three suppositions—

a That the increase is fictitious and due to doctors having mistaken lung cancer for other diseases in the earlier part of this century. This cannot be true since the rise has been far greater in men than in women and there is no difference in the accuracy of diagnosis of the cause of death in men and women.

b That the rising death rate from lung cancer may be a consequence of the falling death rate from tuberculosis [12]. There is nothing to support this hypothesis. It is notable that while the fall in tuberculosis mortality has been greater in women than in men, the rise in lung cancer has been greater in men.

c That increasing air pollution by coal smoke is responsible [28]. Such pollution has in fact been declining while deaths from lung cancer have gone up, and the relation of air pollution to lung cancer mortality is unimpressive compared with that to cigarette smoking [65].

4. 28   There are other objections to the genetic hypothesis. It demands a very close quantitative relationship of inherited liability to lung cancer with inherited liability to smoking a particular quantity of cigarettes, to starting at a particular age, to degree of inhalation, to variations in ways of smoking (paras 4. 7 to 4. 9), to a tendency to switch to filter-tipped cigarettes, and to both the cessation of smoking and the duration of abstinence. All these factors are, on the other hand, consistent with the hypothesis that exposure of the bronchial tubes to cigarette smoke heightens the risk of developing lung cancer and that the greater the exposure the greater is the risk.

Conclusion

4. 29   The quantitative association between cigarette smoking and the development of lung cancer is most simply explained on a causal basis and no other explanation accounts for the facts. The suffering, shortening of life and unhappiness from this disease to tens of thousands of people and their families every year in this country, and to hundreds of thousands of people in other countries, can be prevented only by abstention from smoking cigarettes. Some reduction of the present toll of life would probably result if those who must continue to smoke were to adopt the less hazardous habits referred to in para 9. 47.

4. 30   If in England and Wales there is no change in the numbers or kind of cigarettes smoked, it has been forecast from present trends that male deaths from lung cancer will level off in the 1980s at some 35,000 to 40,000 per annum [71]. At that time the female deaths will probably have reached about 10,000 to 15,000 per annum, so that the total loss of life from lung cancer will be between 45,000 and 55,000 every year. While most of this increase will occur in older people at least one third of these deaths will be in people under the age of 65.

4. 31   If, on the other hand, cigarette smoking were to cease in this country the death rate from lung cancer would soon begin to fall and eventually, within some twenty years, would sink to one-fifth or, among men, to one-tenth of its present level. The total number of deaths in both sexes would then be less than 5,000 each year. This is a formidable contrast between two realistic forecasts.

REFERENCES

1. ABELIN, T., and GSELL, O. R. (1967). 'Relative risk of pulmonary cancer in cigar and pipe smokers.' *Cancer, N.Y.,* **20,** 1288.

2. AUERBACH, O., STOUT, A. P., HAMMOND, E. C., and GARFINKEL, L. (1961). 'Changes in bronchial epithelium in relation to cigarette smoking and in relation to lung cancer.' *New Engl. J. Med.,* **265,** 253. (1962). 'Changes in bronchial epithelium in relation to sex, age, residence, smoking and pneumonia.' *New Engl. J. Med.* **267,** 111.

3. AUERBACH, O., STOUT, A. P., HAMMOND, E. C., and GARFINKEL, L. (1962). 'Bronchial epithelium in former smokers.' *New Engl. J. Med.*, **267**, 119.

4. AUERBACH, O., STOUT, A. P., HAMMOND, E. C., and GARFINKEL, L. (1967). 'Multiple primary bronchial carcinomas.' *Cancer, N.Y.*, **20**, 699.

5. BEFFINGER, J. (1965). Unpublished communication quoted in: Eysenck, H. J. *Smoking, Health and Personality* (reference 28), p. 133.

6. BERKSON, J. (1963). 'Smoking and lung cancer.' *Am. Statistn.*, **17**, 15.

7. BEST, E. W. R. (1966). *A Canadian study of smoking and health.* Department of National Health and Welfare, Ottawa, p. 137.

8. BIDSTRUP, P. L., and CASE, R. A. M. (1956). 'Carcinoma of the lung in workmen in the bichromate producing industry in Great Britain.' *Br. J. ind. Med.*, **13**, 260.

9. BRETT, G. Z., and BENJAMIN, B. (1968). 'Smoking habits of men employed in industry and mortality.' *Br. med. J.*, **3**, 82.

10. BRITISH MEDICAL JOURNAL (1966). 'Cough and Cancer', **2**, 903.

11. BROSS, I. D. J., and GIBSON, R. (1968). 'Risks of lung cancer in smokers who switch to filter cigarettes.' *Am. J. publ. Hlth.*, **58**, 1396.

12. BROWNLEE, K. A. (1965). 'A review of "Smoking and Health".' *J. Am. statist. Ass.*, **60**, 722.

13. CAMPBELL, A. H., and LEE, E. J. (1963). 'The relationship between lung cancer and chronic bronchitis.' *Br. J. Dis. Chest*, **57**, 113.

14. CASE, R. A. M., and LEE, A. J. (1955). 'Mustard gas poisoning, chronic bronchitis and lung cancer; an investigation into the the possibility that poisoning by mustard gas in the 1914–18 war might be a factor in the production of neoplasia.' *Br. J. prev. soc. Med.*, **9**, 62.

15. CHANG, S. C. (1957). 'Microscopic properties of whole mounts and sections of human bronchial epithelium of smokers and non-smokers.' *Cancer, N.Y.*, **10**, 1246.

16. CLEMMESEN, J. (1965). *Statistical Studies in the Aetiology of Malignant Neoplasms. I. Review and Results.* Munksgaard, Copenhagen. p. 189.

17. COHEN, J., and HEIMANN, R. K. (1962). 'Heavy smokers with low mortality.' *Ind. Med. Surg.*, **31**, 115.

18. CORNFIELD, J., HAENSZEL, W., HAMMOND, E. C., LILIENFELD, A. M., SHIMKIN, M. B., and WYNDER, E. L. (1959). 'Smoking and lung cancer. Recent evidence and a discussion of some questions.' *J. natn. Cancer Inst.*, **22**, 173.

19. DANISH JOINT COMMITTEE (1962). 'Tobacco and lung cancer.' *Dan. med. Bull.*, **9**, 97.

20. DARK, J., O'CONNOR, M., PEMBERTON, M., and RUSSELL, M. H. (1963). 'Relighting of cigarettes and lung cancer.' *Br. med. J.*, **2**, 1164.

21. DENOIX, P. F., SCHWARTZ, D., and ANGUERA, G. (1958). 'L'enquete française sur l'etiologie du cancer broncho-pulmonaire, analyse detaillée.' *Bull. Ass. fr. Etude Cancer*, **45**, 1.

22. DOLL, R. (1958). 'Cancer of the lung and nose in nickel workers.' *Br. J. ind. Med.*, **15**, 217.

23. DOLL, R. (1959). 'Occupational lung cancer: a review.' *Br. J. ind. Med.*, **16**, 181.

24. DOLL, R. (1969). 'The geographical distribution of cancer.' *Br. J. Cancer*, **23**, 1.

25. DOLL, R., FISHER, R. E. W., GAMMON, E. J., GUNN, W., HUGHES, G. O., TYRER, F. H., and WILSON, W. (1965). 'Mortality of gasworkers with special reference to cancers of the lung and bladder, chronic bronchitis and pneumoconiosis.' *Br. J. ind. Med.*, **22**, 1.

26a. DOLL, R., and HILL, A. B. (1964). 'Mortality in relation to smoking: ten years observations of British doctors.' *Br. med. J.*, **1**, 1399 and 1460.

26b. DOLL, R., and PIKE, M. C. (1970). Personal communication.

27. DOLL, R., HILL, A. B., GRAY, P. G., and PARR, E. A. (1959). 'Lung cancer mortality and the length of cigarette ends.' *Brit. med. J.*, **1**, 322.

28. EYSENCK, H. J. (1965). *Smoking, Health and Personality*. Weidenfeld and Nicolson, London.

29. FISHER, R. A. (1958). 'Lung cancer and cigarettes?' *Nature, Lond.*, **182**, 108 and 596.

30. FISHER, R. A. (1959). *Smoking: the Cancer Controversy*. Oliver and Boyd, Edinburgh.

31. FRIBERG, L., KAIJ, L., DENCKER, S. J., and JONSSON, E. (1959). 'Smoking habits of monozygotic and dizygotic twins.' *Br. med. J.*, **1**, 1090.

32. GILSON, J. C. (1966). 'Health hazards of asbestos: recent studies on its biological effects.' *Trans. Soc. occup. Med.*, **16**, 62.

33. GRAHAM, S. (1968). 'Cancer of lung related to smoking behaviour.' *Cancer, N.Y.*, **21**, 523.

34. HARCOURT KITCHIN, C. (1966). *You may Smoke*. Library 33 Limited, London.

35. HAMMOND, E. C. (1958). 'Lung cancer death rates in England and Wales compared with those in the USA. *Brit. med. J.*, **2**, 649.

36. HAMMOND, E. C. (1966). 'Smoking in relation to the death rates of one million men and women.' *Nat. Cancer Inst. Monogr.*, **19**, 127.

37. HAMMOND, E. C., and HORN, D. (1958). 'Smoking and death rates—report on forty-four month of follow up of 187,783 men. II Death rates by cause.' *J. Am. med. Ass.*, **166**, 1294.

38. HARDY, D. R. (1968). 'Smoking and Health. The importance of objectivity.' In *Smoking, Health and Behaviour*. Ed. Borgatta, E. F., and Evans, R. R. Aldine Publishing Co., Chicago. p. 41.

39. HUEPER, W. C. (1966). a, Discussion, p. 192: b, 'Cancer and occupation: a methodologic study.' In *Krebs—Documentation und statistik maligner Tumoren*. Ed. G. Wagner. F. K. Schatter Verlag, Stuttgart.

40. HUEPER, W. C., and CONWAY, W. D. (1964). *Chemical Carcinogenesis and Cancers*. Charles C. Thomas, Springfield Illinois.

41. IDE, G., SUNTZEFF, V., and COWDREY, E. V. (1959). 'Comparison of the histopathology of tracheal and bronchial epithelium of smokers and non-smokers.' *Cancer, N.Y.*, **12**, 473.

42. JONES, D. L. (1966). 'An epidemiological study of certain aspects of lung cancer in New South Wales.' *Med. J. Austr.*, **1**, 765.

43. KAHN, H. A. (1966). 'The Dorn study of smoking and mortality among US veterans: Report on eight and one-half years of observation.' *Natn. Cancer Inst. Monogr.*, **19**, 1, 1.

44. KISSEN, D. M., and EYSENCK, H. J. (1962). 'Personality in male lung cancer patients.' *J. psychosom. Res.*, **6**, 123.

45. KOLLER, S. (1964). 'Bemerkungen zu der Arbeit von R. Poche, O. Mittman und O. Kneller.' *Z. Krebsforsch*, **66**, 187.

46. LAMB, D. (1967). 'Histological changes in the tracheobronchial epithelium of rats exposed to tobacco smoke' (abstract). *Thorax*, **22**, 290.

47. LARSON, P. S., and SILVETTE, H. (1968). *Tobacco experimental and clinical studies. Supplement* 1. The Williams Wilkins Co., Baltimore. *a*, 513; *b*, 523.

48. LEE, A. M., and FRAUMENI, J. F., Jr. (1969). 'Arsenic and respiratory cancer in man: an occupational study.' *J. natn. Cancer Inst.*, **42**, 1045.

49. LE SHAN, L. (1959). 'Psychological states as factors in the development of malignant disease: a critical review.' *J. natn. Cancer Inst.*, **22**, 1.

50. MALLAN, LLOYD. (1966). *It is Safe to Smoke*. Hawthorn Books, Inc., New York City.

51. McKENNELL, A. C. and THOMAS, R. K. (1967). *Adults' and Adolescents' Smoking Habits and Attitudes*. A report on a survey carried out for the Ministry of Health. SS 353/B, HMSO, London.

52. MEDICAL RESEARCH COUNCIL (1957). 'Tobacco smoking and cancer of the lung.' HMSO *Br. med. J.*, **1**, 1523.

53. MINISTER OF HEALTH (1957). 'Government action on smoking and lung cancer.' *Br. med. J.*, **2**, 49.

54. MYDDELTON, G. (1965). Carcinoma of bronchus (letter). *Lancet*, **2**, 796.

55. NASIELL, M. (1968). 'Sputum—cytologic changes in smokers and non-smokers in relation to chronic inflammatory lung diseases.' *Acta path. microbiol. scand.*, **74**, 205.

56. NATIONAL CANCER INSTITUTE OF CANADA (1958). 'Lung cancer and smoking.' *Can. med. Ass. J.*, **79**, 566.

57. NETHERLANDS MINISTRY OF SOCIAL AFFAIRS AND PUBLIC HEALTH. (1957). The Hague: Press Notice No. 1233 and *Ned. Tijdschr. Geneesk*, **101**, 459.

58. PASCUA, M. (1952). 'The evolution of mortality in Europe during the twentieth century: Cancer mortality.' *Epidem. vit. Statist. Rep.*, **5**, 1.

59. PASCUA, M. (1955). 'Increased mortality from cancer of the respiratory system.' *Bull. Wld. Hlth. Org.*, **12**, 687.

60. POCHE, R., MITTMANN, O., and KNELLER, O. (1964). 'Statistiche Untersuchungen uber das Bronchial-carcinom in Nordrhein-Westfalen.' *Z. Krebsforsch*, **66**, 87 and 250.

61. RAASCHOU-NIELSEN, E. (1960). 'Smoking habits in twins.' *Dan. med. Bull.*, **7**, 82.

62. RANDIG, K. (1955). 'Zur Atiologie der Lungenkrebses.' *Dt. med. Wschr.*, **80**. 718.

63. RIMINGTON, J. (1968). 'Smoking, sputum and lung cancer.' *Brit. med. J.*, **1**, 732.

64. ROYAL COLLEGE OF PHYSICIANS (1962). *Smoking and Health*. A report of the Royal College of Physicians on smoking in relation to cancer of the lung and other diseases. Pitman Medical, London.

65. ROYAL COLLEGE OF PHYSICIANS (1970). *Air Pollution and Health*. Pitman Medical, London. Chapter 6.

66. SANDERUD, K. (1958). 'Squamous metaplasia of the respiratory tract epithelium.' *Acta. path. microbiol. scand.*, **43**, 47.

67. SEGI, M., and KURIHARA, M. (1966). *Cancer Mortality from Selected Sites in 24 Countries. No. 4, 1962–63.* Department of Public Health, Tohoku University, Sendai, Japan.

68. SELIKOFF, I. J., HAMMOND, E. C., and CHURG, J. (1968). 'Asbestos exposure, smoking and neoplasia.' *J. Am. med. Ass.*, **204**, 106.

69. SELTZER, C. C. (1963). 'Morphologic constitution and smoking.' *J. Am. med. Ass.*, **183**, 639.

70. SMOKING AND HEALTH (1967). A statement approved by the Executive Committee of the American Thoracic Society. *Am. Rev. resp. Dis.*, **96**, 613.

71. SPRINGETT, V. H. (1966). 'The beginning of the end of the increase in mortality from carcinoma of the lung.' *Thorax*, **21**, 132.

72. THOMAS, C. B. (1960). 'Characteristics of smokers compared with non-smokers in a population of healthy young adults, including observations on family history, blood pressure, heart rate, body weight, cholesterol and certain psychologic traits.' *Ann. intern. Med.*, **53**, 697.

73. TODD, G. F. (1969). *Statistics of smoking in the United Kingdom.* Tobacco Research Council Research Paper 1. 5th edit.

74. TODD, G. F., and MASON, J. I. (1959). 'Concordance of smoking habits in monozygotic and dizygotic twins.' *Heredity, Lond.*, **13**, 417.

75. TOKUHATA, G. K., and LILIENFELD, A. M. (1963). 'Familial aggregation of lung cancer in humans.' *J. natn. Cancer Inst.*, **30**, 289.

76. US PUBLIC HEALTH SERVICE. SURGEON GENERAL'S ADVISORY COMMITTEE ON SMOKING AND HEALTH (1964). *Smoking and Health.* Public Health Service Publication No. 1103. *a*, pp. 150–160; *b*, pp. 161–167; *c*, pp. 180–182; *d*, p. 188.

77. VAN DER WAL, A. M., HUIZINGA, E., ORIE, N. G. M., SLUITER, H. J., and DE VRIES, K. (1966). 'Cancer and chronic non-specific lung disease (CNSLD).' *Scand. J. resp. Dis.*, **47**, 161.

78. WADA, S., YAMADA, A., NISHMOTO, Y., TOKUOKA, S., MIYANISHI, M., KATSUTA, A., and UMISA, M. (1963). 'Neoplasm of the respiratory tract in poison gas workers.' *J. Hiroshima med. Ass.*, **16**, 728.

79. WAGONER, J. K., ARCHER, V. E., LUNDIN, F. E., Jr., HOLADAY, D. A., and LLOYD, J. W. (1965). 'Radiation as the cause of lung cancer among uranium miners.' *New Engl. J. Med.*, **273**, 181.

80. WAINGROW, S. M., HORN, D,. and IKARD, F. F. (1968). 'Dosage pattern of cigarette smoking in American adults.' *Am. J. publ. Hlth.*, **58**, 54.

81. WALLER, R. E. (1965). Carcinoma of bronchus (letter), *Lancet*, **2**, 953.

82. WICKEN, A. J. (1966). *Environmental and Personal Factors in Lung Cancer and Bronchitis Mortality in Northern Ireland, 1960–62.* Tobacco Research Council. Research Paper 9.

83. WORLD HEALTH ORGANISATION (1960). 'Epidemiology of cancer of the lung. Report of a study group.' *Wld. Hlth. Org. techn. Rep. Ser.*, 192.

84. YERUSHALMY, J. (1962). 'Statistical considerations and evaluation of epidemiological evidence.' In *Tobacco and Health*, ed. G. James and T. Rosenthal. C. C. Thomas, Springfield, Illinois. p. 208.

5. Smoking, Chronic Bronchitis and Emphysema

5. 1   Each year in the United Kingdom over 30,000 men and women die from bronchitis and emphysema after years of disability. The number of deaths attributed to these diseases in people aged 35 to 64 in the United Kingdom in 1968 was nearly 6,500 in men and 1,500 in women. This was respectively 6·6 and 2·6 per cent of all deaths in each sex at these ages (Table 4. 1). The bronchitis death rate rises steeply in older people, but it is during the years before retirement that avoidable deaths are so to be deplored. The average number of working days lost each year through sickness-absence due to bronchitis is now about 35 million—ten or twelve times the number of days lost through industrial disputes. The importance of cigarette smoking in the development of every stage of chronic bronchitis is becoming increasingly clear.

5. 2   The first symptoms of chronic bronchitis are a cough and expectoration of phlegm, usually dismissed as a 'smoker's cough' and regarded by many smokers as quite normal.* The sputum coughed up is usually clear, but at times, particularly during the winter, it becomes more profuse and contains yellow or green pus; the patient then usually has a fever and feels ill. The most serious feature of the disease is progressive, persistent narrowing of the airways in the lungs. This causes increasing difficulty in breathing, which is often made worse by an associated emphysema. In this condition the minute air sacs in the lung, where oxygen is taken up by the blood, break down into larger air spaces so that the area available

---

* When patients with bronchitis are asked if they have a cough they not infrequently reply, 'yes, like everyone else'. They do not realise that people with healthy lungs have no cough and produce no phlegm.

for gas exchange is reduced. When this happens much more air has to be breathed to supply the oxygen needs of the body. Severe shortness of breath on slight exertion causes much distress. In some patients circulation of the blood through the lungs is also impeded and finally the heart may fail.

Cough with Sputum Caused by Cigarette Smoking

5. 3   Surveys in many countries have shown a close relationship in both men and women between the numbers of cigarettes smoked and the frequency of cough with expectoration [2, 3, 16, 18–21, 28–32, 35, 43, 44, 46–48, 50, 51, 57–59, 61, 69]. This has also been found in school children [29]: indeed, the frequency of cough and phlegm among teenagers who smoke more than five cigarettes a day is only slightly less than among adult cigarette smokers. That cigarette smoke is the main cause of cough and phlegm is shown by the fact that these symptoms usually diminish or disappear when cigarette smoking is given up [19, 23, 67].

Cigarette Smoking and Recurrent Chest Illness

5. 4   Normal bronchial tubes are free from bacteria, which are, however, found in the bronchi of subjects with bronchitis [9, 10, 40–42]. Cigarette smoke causes excessive production of mucus that interferes with the defences of the lung against infection [22, 60] so that cigarette smokers, particularly those with a cough, have an increased frequency of chest illnesses [18, 19]. The susceptibility is found not only in older people but also in young people such as undergraduates and student nurses who smoke [26, 50]. Although these illnesses may be regarded by people without severe lung damage as only a nuisance, they are often treated with expensive antibiotics, and cause much absence from work. As chronic bronchitis progresses and lung function becomes impaired, these illnesses become increasingly serious and may ultimately be fatal.

Cigarette Smoking and Impairment of Lung Function

5. 5   The function of the lungs has been shown to be, on average, in every respect less efficient in cigarette smokers

than in non-smokers of the same age [16, 18, 19, 28–32, 36, 54, 55, 56, 59, 62, 63, 67, 68–70, 71]. The chief abnormality is progressive resistance to the flow of air in the smaller bronchial tubes, which causes gradually increasing difficulty in breathing. There is also interference with the ability of the lungs to transfer oxygen from the inspired air to the blood. This impairment of gas transfer has been demonstrated in smokers of all ages [54]; even in young smokers the blood leaving the lungs may contain less oxygen than normal [62, 63].

Bronchitis Less Frequent in Pipe or Cigar Smokers

5. 6 An invariable finding in bronchitis surveys is that cough and expectoration, recurrent chest illnesses, and impaired lung function affect pipe and cigar smokers much less often than cigarette smokers, and only slightly more often than non-smokers. Cigarette smokers who change to smoking only pipes or cigars may find that they cough less. It has not yet been shown whether this change improves the impaired function of the lungs.

Benefits of Stopping Smoking Cigarettes

5. 7 When cigarette smokers stop smoking their cough and phlegm usually diminish and they become less liable to chest infections [19, 23]. In younger smokers lung function may rapidly return to normal [36, 52, 62, 67]. In moderately affected patients, giving up cigarettes may greatly relieve breathlessness despite years of smoking. When bronchitis or emphysema is advanced, however, the damage to the lungs is irreversible, so that stopping smoking can have little effect on breathlessness, although much relief comes from diminution of cough and phlegm [11, 33].

Changes in Lung Structure

5. 8 Post-mortem studies of the lungs of men whose smoking habits have been recorded show enlargement and overactivity of the glands in the bronchial tubes that produce mucus [1, 6, 45, 65]. Destruction of the lung by emphysema also increases with increasing numbers of cigarettes smoked [7, 53].

Smoking and Deaths from Chronic Bronchitis and Emphysema

5. 9   Several recent reports have confirmed that death rates from these diseases rise with cigarette consumption [8, 15, 17, 24, 34]. In the survey of British doctors, deaths from bronchitis among those who had smoked twenty-five or more cigarettes daily were over twenty times more common than among non-smokers. Deaths from bronchitis in pipe and cigar smokers were only slightly more than in non-smokers. The findings in the American [34] and Canadian veterans [8] studies were similar (Figure 5. 1).

5. 10   In view of the association between deaths from bronchitis and numbers of cigarettes smoked it might have been expected that rising cigarette smoking in the past few decades would have caused a steep increase in deaths from bronchitis

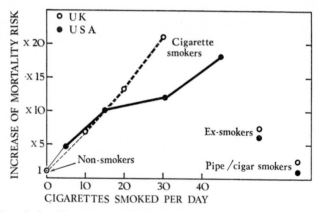

Figure 5. 1   *The increase of death rates from bronchitis in men who smoke various numbers of cigarettes, who have stopped smoking and in those who smoke only pipes or cigars.* This figure may be compared with Figure 4. 2 and shows how much the risk of dying from bronchitis or emphysema is multiplied by smoking cigarettes in various quantities when compared with the risk of non-smokers. It also shows the risk in those who used to smoke and in pipe or cigar smokers. The figures are derived from Doll and Hill's study of British doctors [17] and from Dorn's study of American veterans [34]. The slightly lower risk of the American men may, as in the case of lung cancer, be due to the longer stub length left by American smokers and the lower levels of air pollution in America. The reduced risk for men who have stopped smoking and the very small risk of men who smoke only pipes or cigars is clear.

similar to that from lung cancer; but this has not happened. These contrasting mortality trends are illustrated in Figure 5. 2. Table 5. 1, however, shows that during this century changes in the ratio of male to female deaths from cancer of the lung and bronchitis have been similar. The most likely explanation is that, while social improvements and advances in treatment have tended to reduce the frequency and severity of bronchitis in both sexes, these benefits have been cancelled

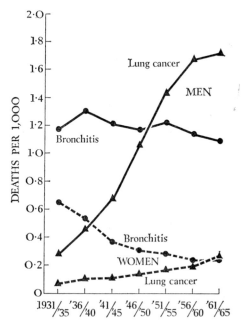

Figure 5. 2 *Death rates from lung cancer and bronchitis in men and women aged 45–64 in England and Wales 1931–1965.* Death rates from lung cancer have risen steeply in men and much less steeply in women during this period. Death rates from bronchitis in men have remained almost constant while in women they have declined. The *relative* changes in the two sexes have thus been similar (Table 5. 1), men being progressively more often affected than women in respect of both diseases. This sex difference is consistent with the greater increase of cigarette consumption by men during the past fifty years. The difference between trends for the two diseases is related to various factors which have improved the outlook for patients with bronchitis but which have had no effect on the more fatal disease, lung cancer.

TABLE 5. 1

Ratios of mortality between men and women aged 45 to 64 for lung cancer and bronchitis in England and Wales 1916–1965

Period	Lung Cancer	Bronchitis
1916–20	1·7	1·2
1921–25	2·1	1·2
1926–30	2·7	1·4
1931–35	3·6	1·8
1936–40	4·4	2·5
1941–45	5·4	3·3
1946–50	6·6	3·9
1951–55	7·5	4·4
1956–60	7·6	5·1
1961–65	7·2	5·0

out in men because they smoke so many more cigarettes; and so the male death rate remains constant. There is no evidence of an increase in occupational bronchitis or any increased exposure of men to air pollution which could account for these trends. Women are probably not much less susceptible to bronchitis than men since in men and women of similar smoking habits bronchitic symptoms have been found to be equally frequent or only slightly less frequent in women [14, 39, 49]. Probably because they start smoking at a later age and inhale less (paras 1. 6 and 4. 21) women have a rather lower bronchitis death rate than men who smoke the same number of cigarettes [24, 66].

Effect of Stopping Smoking on Deaths from Bronchitis and Emphysema

5. 11   In both British and American prospective studies death rates from bronchitis and emphysema in ex-smokers were similar to those of light cigarette smokers and below the rate for all cigarette smokers (Figure 5. 1). Among British doctors the decline in death rates after cessation of smoking was apparent only in those who had stopped for over five years. This is not surprising, because when the lungs have been severely damaged by bronchitis or emphysema, giving up cigarettes can have little effect on the progress of the

disease [11, 33]. Nevertheless British doctors, many of whom have stopped smoking in the past twenty years, have shown a more favourable trend of bronchitis mortality than all British men between the ages of 35 and 64 when serious lung damage is less frequent than in older men (Table 2. 3).

Cigarette Smoking as a Cause of Bronchitis and Emphysema

5. 12   There is little doubt that the greatly increased risk of illness, disability, and death from chronic bronchitis and emphysema in cigarette smokers is due to their exposure to the smoke rather than to any constitutional factor that might cause both liability to chest disease and an increased desire to smoke cigarettes. In identical twins with different smoking habits respiratory symptoms are more frequent and respiratory function is poorer on average in the heavier smoking twins of each pair [12, 44]. In one large American survey in which heavy cigarette smokers were matched with non-smokers in relation to a large number of factors such as race, religion, and personal habits, which might indicate constitutional differences, the smokers still had a much higher death rate from bronchitis and emphysema [25].

5. 13   Animal experiments have confirmed that cigarette smoke can induce bronchitis. Changes similar to those found in patients with severe bronchitis occur in rats exposed to tobacco smoke [38], and dogs regularly exposed to cigarette smoke also develop bronchitis and emphysema [4, 5, 27].

Other Causes of Bronchitis

5. 14   While cigarette smoking is a major cause of chronic bronchitis, it is not the only one.

a   Bronchitis seems to have been an important cause of death in this country before cigarette smoking was common. The mortality rate from the disease fell steadily during the earlier part of this century until it reached its present constant level in men and slow rate of decline in women. Deaths attributed to bronchitis are more frequent in the British Isles than anywhere else in the world, even in countries with equally high consumption of cigarettes.

Surveys in the USA and Scandinavia have shown that smokers in those countries have less bronchitis than British smokers [13, 31, 46, 47]. The Report on Air Pollution by the Royal College of Physicians concluded that life-long exposure to air heavily polluted by coal smoke in particular contributes to the special liability of British cigarette smokers to develop severe bronchitis. That other unidentified factors in the British environment may increase this risk is indicated by the observation that the prevalence of bronchitis in British rural areas is greater than in rural or even urban areas in, for instance, Scandinavia, Finland, and the USA [31, 32, 46, 47].

b In some occupations with heavy exposure to dust the rate of bronchitis is higher than in the general population [43]. In some studies this difference between men exposed and not exposed to dust has been found chiefly in cigarette smokers [21, 58, 59].

c Deaths from bronchitis in unskilled labourers and their wives (social class V) are five times more frequent than in professional men and their wives (social class I) although there has until the last few years been little social class gradient in cigarette smoking. The reason for this great difference between the social classes in the severity of bronchitis remains obscure.

5. 15   The fact that cigarette smokers are more affected than others by air pollution and dusty work indicates that their damaged lungs are less able to withstand the effect of various other factors which may increase the severity of bronchitis and emphysema.

5. 16   Since many life-long smokers remain free from serious chest disease those affected must have some special liability to the injurious effects of cigarette smoke. There is some evidence that this susceptibility may be inherited [12, 64]. If these individuals could be detected early in life before irreversible changes had taken place their disablement might be prevented. In British working men it was found that cigarette smokers with even mild impairment of lung function were more liable to progressive lung disease over a seven year

period than were those with normal function, whether or not they had cough and phlegm [19]. This implies that general practitioners or industrial medical officers, using simple tests of lung function might detect apparently healthy but susceptible subjects who, if they were to abstain from cigarettes, should not develop grave respiratory disease.

Conclusion

5. 17 Cigarette smoking is today a most important predisposing cause of chronic bronchitis and the emphysema that so often accompanies it, although other factors increase the liability of cigarette smokers to develop these diseases. If modern cigarettes were no longer smoked there would ultimately be a great economic saving to industry from reduced sickness absence and to the exchequer from costly treatment. The distressing disablement of thousands of men and women which precedes death from these diseases would also be much less.

REFERENCES

1. ANDERSON, A. E., Jr., HERNANDEZ, J. A., HOLMES, W. L., and FORAKER, A. G. (1966). 'Pulmonary emphysema. Prevalence, severity and anatomical patterns in macrosections, with respect to smoking habits.' *Archs. envir. Hlth.*, **12**, 569.

2. ANDERSON, D. O., and FERRIS, B. G. (1962). 'Role of tobacco smoking in the causation of chronic respiratory disease.' *New Engl. J. Med.*, **267**, 787.

3. ANDERSON, D. O., FERRIS, B. G., and ZICKMANTEL, R. (1965). 'The Chilliwack Respiratory Survey, 1963, Part IV. The effect of tobacco smoking on the prevalence of respiratory disease.' *Can. med. Ass. J.*, **92**, 1066.

4. AUERBACH, O., HAMMOND, E. C., KIRMAN, D., and GARFINKEL, L. (1967). 'Emphysema produced in dogs by cigarette smoking.' *J. Am. med. Ass.*, **199**, 241.

5. AUERBACH, O., HAMMOND, E. C., KIRMAN, D., GARFINKEL, L., and STOUT, A. P. (1967). 'Histologic changes in bronchial tubes of cigarette smoking dogs.' *Cancer, N.Y.*, **20**, 2055.

6. AUERBACH, O., STOUT, A. P. HAMMOND, E. C., and GARFINKEL, L. (1962). 'Changes in bronchial epithelium in relation to sex, age, residence, smoking and pneumonia.' *New Engl. J. Med.*, **267**, 111.

7 AUERBACH, O., STOUT, A. P., HAMMOND, E. C., and GARFINKEL, L. (1963). 'Smoking habits and age in relation to pulmonary changes. Rupture of alveolar septums, fibrosis and thickening of walls of small arteries and arterioles.' *New Engl. J. Med.*, **269**, 1045.

8. BEST, E. W. R. (1966). *Canadian Study of Smoking and Health.* Ottawa Department of National Health and Welfare.

9. BROWN, C. C., COLEMAN, M. B., ALLEY, R. D., STRANAHAN, A., and STUART HARRIS, C. H. (1954). 'Chronic bronchitis and emphysema. Significance of bacterial flora in the sputum.' *Am. J. Med.,* **17,** 478.

10. BRUMFITT, W., WILLOUGHBY, M. L. N., and BROMLEY, L. L. (1957). 'An evaluation of sputum examination in chronic bronchitis.' *Lancet,* **2,** 1306.

11. BURROWS, B., and EARLE, R. H. (1969). 'Course and prognosis of chronic obstructive lung disease. A prospective study of 200 patients.' *New Engl. J. Med.,* **280,** 397.

12. CEDERLOF, R., FRIBERG, L., JONSSON, E., and KAIJ, L. (1965). 'Morbidity among monozygotic twins.' *Archs. envir Hlth.,* **10,** 346.

13. CHRISTENSEN, O. W., and WOOD, C. H. (1958). 'Bronchitis mortality rates in England and Wales and in Denmark.' *Br. med. J.,* **1,** 620.

14. COLLEGE OF GENERAL PRACTITIONERS (1961). 'Chronic bronchitis in Great Britain.' A national survey carried out by the Respiratory Disease Section of the College of General Practitioners. *Br. med. J.,* **2,** 973.

15. DEAN, G. (1966). 'Lung cancer and bronchitis in Northern Ireland 1960–62.' *Brit. med. J.,* **1,** 1506.

16. DENSEN, P. M., JONES, E. W., BASS, H. E., and BREUER, J. A. (1967). 'A survey of respiratory disease among New York City postal and transit workers.' *Envir. Res.,* **1,** 262.

17. DOLL, R., and HILL, A. B. (1964). 'Mortality in relation to smoking: ten years observations of British doctors.' *Br. med. J.,* **1,** 1399 and 1460.

18. FLETCHER, C. M., ELMES, P. C., FAIRBAIRN, A. S., and WOOD, C. H. (1959). 'The significance of respiratory symptoms and the diagnosis of chronic bronchitis in a working population.' *Br. med. J.,* **2,** 257.

19. FLETCHER, C. M., TINKER, C. M., SPEIZER, F. E. and PETRO, R. (1971). A follow-up study of the natural history of obstructive bronchitis. Bronchitis III. Ed. Orie, N. G. M., and Sluiter, H. J. Royal Vancorum Assen. Holland. (In the press.)

20. FREOUR, P., and COUDRAY, P. (1967). 'Étude épidémiologique des troubles, broncho-respiratoires dans une grande agglomeration urbaine.' *Bull. Inst. natn. Sante Recherché méd.,* **22,** 901.

21. GANDEVIA, B., and MILNE, J. (1965). 'Ventilatory capacity on exposure to jute dust and the relevance of productive cough and smoking to the response.' *Br. J. ind. Med.,* **22,** 187.

22. GREEN, G. M., and CAROLIN, D. (1967). 'The depressant effect of cigarette smoke on the *in vitro* antibacterial activity of alveolar macrophages.' *New Engl. J. Med.,* **276,** 421.

23. HAMMOND, E. C. (1965). 'Evidence on the effects of giving up smoking.' *Am. J. publ. Hlth.,* **55,** 682.

24. HAMMOND, E. C. (1966). 'Smoking in relation to the death rate of one million men and women.' *Natn. Cancer Inst. Monogr.,* **19,** 127.

25. HAMMOND, E. C. (1964). 'Smoking in relation to mortality and morbidity. Findings in first thirty-four months of follow-up in a prospective study started in 1959.' *J. natn. Cancer Inst.,* **32,** 1161.

26. HAYNES, W. F., Jr., KRSTULOVIC, V. J., and LOOMIS BELL, A. L., Jr. (1966). 'Smoking habit and incidence of respiratory tract infections in a group of adolescent males.' *Am. Rev. resp. Dis.*, **93**, 730.

27. HERNANDEZ, J. A., ANDERSON, A. E., HOLMES, W. L., and FORAKER, A. G. (1966). 'Pulmonary parenchymal defects in dogs following prolonged cigarette smoke exposure.' *Am. Rev. resp. Dis.*, **93**, 78.

28. HIGGINS, I. T. T. (1959). 'Tobacco smoking, respiratory symptoms and ventilatory capacity. Studies in random samples of the population.' *Br. med. J.*, **1**, 325.

29. HOLLAND, W. W., and ELLIOTT, A. (1968). 'Cigarette smoking, respiratory symptoms and anti-smoking propaganda. An experiment.' *Lancet*, **1**, 41.

30. HOLLAND, W. W., and REID, D. D. (1965). 'The urban factor in chronic bronchitis.' *Lancet*, **1**, 445.

31. HOLLAND, W. W., REID, D. D., SELTSER, R., and STONE, R. W. (1965). 'Respiratory disease in England and the United States.' *Archs. envir. Hlth.*, **10**, 338.

32. HUHTI, E. (1965). 'Prevalence of respiratory symptoms, chronic bronchitis and pulmonary emphysema in a Finnish rural population.' *Acta tuberc. scand.* Suppl. 61.

33. JONES, N. L., BURROWS, B., and FLETCHER, C. M. (1967). 'Serial studies of 100 patients with chronic airways obstruction in London and Chicago.' *Thorax*, **22**, 327.

34. KAHN, H. A. (1966). 'The Dorn study of smoking and mortality among US veterans. Report on eight and one-half years of observation.' *Natn. Cancer Inst. Monogr.*, **19**, 1.

35. KOURILSKY, R., BRILLE, D., and HATTE, J. (1966). 'Étude statistique de la relation entre le tabac et la bronchite chronique.' *Bull. Acad. natn. Méd.* (Paris), **150**, 318.

36. KRUMHOLZ, R. A., CHEVALIER, R. B., and ROSS, J. C. (1964). 'Cardiopulmonary function in young smokers. A comparison of pulmonary function measurements and some cardio-pulmonary responses to exercise between a group of young smokers and a comparable group of non-smokers.' *Ann. intern. Med.*, **60**, 603, and **62**, 197.

38. LAMB, D., PASSEY, R. D., and REID, L. (1969). 'Goblet cell increase in rat bronchial epithelium after exposure to cigarette and cigar smoke.' *Br. med. J.*, **1**, 33.

39. LAMBERT, P. M., and REID, D. D. (1970). 'Smoking, air pollution and bronchitis in Britain.' *Lancet*, **1**, 853.

40. LAURENZI, G. A., GUARNERI, J. J., and ENDRIGA, R. B. (1965). 'Important determinants in pulmonary resistance to bacterial infection.' *Medna. Thorac.*, **22**, 48.

41. LAURENZI, G. A., POTTER, R. T., and KASS, E. M. (1961). 'Bacteriologic flora of the lower respiratory tract.' *New Engl. J. Med.*, **265**, 1273.

42. LEES, A. W., and McNAUGHT, W. (1959). 'Bacteriology of lower respiratory tract secretions, sputum and upper respiratory tract secretions in "normals" and chronics bronchitics.' *Lancet*, **2**, 1112.

43. LOWE, C. R. (1968). 'Chronic bronchitis and occupation.' *Proc. R. Soc. Med.*, **61**, 98.

44. LUNDMAN, T. (1966). 'Smoking in relation to coronary heart disease and lung function in twins. A co-twin control study.' *Acta. med. scand.*, **180**, Suppl. 445.

45. MEGAHED, G. E., SENNA, G. A., EISSA, M. H., SALEH, S. Z., and EISSA, H. A. (1967). 'Smoking versus infection as the aetiology of mucous gland hypertrophy in chronic bronchitis.' *Thorax*, **22**, 271.

46. MORK, T. (1962). 'A comparative study of respiratory disease in England and Wales and Norway.' *Acta. med. scand.*, **172**, Suppl. 384.

47. OLSEN, H. C., and GILSON, J. C. (1960). 'Respiratory symptoms, bronchitis and ventilatory capacity in men: an Anglo-Danish comparison with special reference to differences in smoking habits.' *Br. med. J.*, **1**, 450.

48. OSHIMA, Y., ISHIZAKI, T., MIYAMOTO, T., KABE, J., and MAKINO, S. (1964). 'A study of asthma among Japanese.' *Am. Rev. resp. Dis.*, **90**, 632.

49. OSWALD, N. C., and MEDVEI, V. C. (1955). 'Chronic bronchitis; the effect of cigarette smoking.' *Lancet*, **2**, 843.

50. PARNELL, J. L., ANDERSON, D. O., and KINNIS, C. (1966). 'Cigarette smoking and respiratory infections in a class of student nurses.' *New Engl. J. Med.*, **274**, 979.

51. PETERS, J. M., and FERRIS, B. G. (1967). 'Smoking and morbidity in a college-age groups.' *Am. Rev. resp. Dis.*, **95**, 783.

52. PETERSON, D. I., LONERGAN, L. H., and HARDINGE, M. G. (1968). 'Smoking and pulmonary function.' *Archs. envir. Hlth.*, **16**, 215.

53. PETTY, T. L., RYAN, S. F., and MITCHELL, R. S. (1967). Cigarette smoking and the lungs. Relation to postmortem evidence of emphysema, chronic bronchitis, and black lung pigmentation. *Archs. envir. Hlth.*, **14**, 172.

54. RANKIN, J., GEE, J. B. L., and CHOSY, L. W. (1965). 'The influence of age and smoking on pulmonary diffusing capacity in healthy subjects.' *Medna. Thorac.*, **22**, 366.

55. READ, J., and SELBY, T. (1961). 'Tobacco smoking and ventilatory function of the lungs.' *Br. med. J.*, **2**, 1104.

56. ROSS, J. C., LEY, G. D., KRUMHOLZ, R. A., and RAHBARI, H. (1967). 'A technique for evaluation of gas mixing in the lung- studies in cigarette smokers and non-smokers.' *Am. Rev. resp. Dis.*, **95**, 447.

57. SHARP, J. T., PAUL, O., LEPPER, M. H., McKEAN, H., and SAXTON, G. A. (1965). 'Prevalence of chronic bronchitis in American male urban industrial population.' *Am. Rev. resp. Dis.*, **91**, 510.

58. SLUIS-CREMER, G. K., WALTERS, L. G., and SICHEL, H. S. (1967). 'Chronic bronchitis in miners and non-miners: an epidemiological survey of a community in the gold-mining area of the Transvaal.' *Br. J. ind. Med.*, **24**, 1.

59. SLUIS-CREMER, G. K., WALTERS, L. G., and SICHEL, H. S. (1967). 'Ventilatory function in relation to mining experience and smoking in a random sample of miners and non-miners in a Witwatersrand town.' *Brit. J. ind. Med.*, **24**, 13.

60. SPURGASH, A., EHRLICH, R., and PETZOLD, R. (1968). 'Effect of cigarette smoke on resistance to respiratory infection.' *Archs. envir. Hlth.*, **16**, 385.

61. STANEK, V., FODOR, J., HEJL, Z., WIDIMSKY, J., CHARVAT, P., SANTRUCEK, M., ZAJIC, F., and VAVRIK, M. (1965). 'A contribution to the epidemiology of chronic bronchitis.' *Acta. med. scand.*, **179**, 737.

62. STRIEDER, D. J., and KAZEMI, H. (1967). 'Hypoxemia in young asymptomatic cigarette smokers.' *Ann. thorac. Surg.*, **4**, 523.

63. STRIEDER, D. J., MURPHY, R., and KAZEMI, H. (1968). 'Hypoxaemia in asymptomatic smokers.' *Clin. Res.*, **16**, 376.

64. STUART-HARRIS, C. H. (1965). 'The pathogenesis of chronic bronchitis and emphysema.' *Scott. med. J.*, **10**, 93.

65. THURLBECK, W. M., ANGUS, G. E., and PARE, J. A. P. (1963). 'Mucous gland hypertrophy in chronic bronchitis and its occurrence in smokers.' *Br. J. Dis. Chest*, **57**, 73.

66. WICKEN, A. J. (1966). 'Environmental and personal factors in lung cancer and bronchitis mortality in Northern Ireland, 1960–62.' Tobacco Research Council, Research Paper 9.

67. WILHELMSEN, L. (1967). 'Effects on bronchopulmonary symptoms, ventilation and lung mechanics of abstinence from tobacco smoking.' *Scand. J. resp. Dis.*, **48**, 407.

68. WILHELMSEN, L., and TIBBLIN, G. (1966). 'Tobacco smoking in fifty-year-old men. 1. Respiratory symptoms and ventilatory function tests.' *Scand. J. resp. Dis.*, **47**, 121.

69. WYNDER, E. L., LEMON, F. R., and MANTEL, N. (1965). 'Epidemiology of persistent cough.' *Am. Rev. resp. Dis.*, **91**, 679.

70. ZAMEL, N., YOUSSEF, H. H., and PRIME, F. J. (1963). 'Airway resistance and peak expiratory flow rate in smokers and nonsmokers.' *Lancet*, **1**, 1237.

71. ZWI, S., GOLDMAN, H. I., and LEVIN, A. (1964). 'Cigarette smoking and pulmonary function in healthy young adults.' *Am. Rev. resp. Dis.*, **89**, 73.

72. KRUEGER, D. E., ROGOT, E., BLACKWELDER, W. C., and REID, D. D. (1970). 'The predictive value of a postal questionnaire on cardio-respiratory symptoms.' *J. chron. Dis.* (in press).

6 Smoking and Diseases of the Heart and Blood Vessels

Smoking and Coronary Heart Disease*

6. 1 Coronary heart disease is now a leading cause of death in developed countries. In Britain the number of deaths attributed to it has been rising steadily over the past forty years. Some of the earlier increase was probably the result of growing recognition of the condition (which was first accurately described in 1912) [20] and to ageing of the population (for the death rate rises steeply with advancing age), but much of the continuing increase is real and is not due to changes in diagnostic facilities or in certification of death [31, 32]. Before the age of 50 women are much less commonly affected than men. The large number of middle-aged men now afflicted by coronary disease presents a grave social and economic problem. Of the 99,082 men between the ages of 35 and 64 whose deaths were recorded in the United Kingdom in 1968, 31,013 (31 per cent) died from this form of heart disease; which was also responsible for the death of 7,582 (13 per cent) out of 57,483 women who died in the same year. This may be contrasted with 12,494 deaths in men and 2,543 deaths in women from lung cancer at these ages (Table 4. 1).

* 'Coronary heart disease' is here synonymous with 'coronary artery disease' and 'ischaemic heart disease'. The effects of disease of the coronary arteries (which supply the heart muscle itself with blood) are complex. With advancing age the walls of these arteries (as well as those elsewhere in the body) become encrusted with fatty deposits—a condition known as atheroma. These deposits narrow the arteries and so reduce the flow of blood through them. The blood supply may thus be inadequate when the work of the heart is increased on exertion, and pain may occur in the centre of the chest, to be relieved by rest. This is called 'angina pectoris'. If the blood coagulates (thrombosis) the blood supply to part of the heart is shut off. The heart may stop beating and death may be immediate, either because of an electrical disturbance of the beat or because a large part of the muscle is put out of action. If only a small artery is affected recovery may be complete, but some limitation of effort may persist.

6. 2   Coronary heart disease remains infrequent in under-developed communities which have not adopted the way of life of advanced countries [9], where diet, obesity, lack of exercise, and cigarette smoking have all come under suspicion as causative factors.

6. 3   *Smoking and deaths from coronary heart disease.* All four large prospective studies have shown that the risk of dying from coronary heart disease is greater among cigarette smokers than in non-smokers and smokers of pipes or cigars [7, 13*a*, 18, 22]. The risk is two or three times that of non-

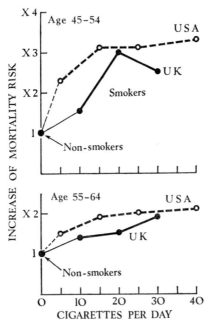

Figure 6. 1   *Increase in death rates from coronary heart disease of males aged 45–64 who smoke various numbers of cigarettes compared with non-smokers of the same ages.* This figure may be compared with Figures 4. 2 and 5. 1. It shows how much the risk of dying from coronary thrombosis is multiplied by smoking cigarettes in various amounts. In the younger men (aged 45–54, upper half of figure) moderate cigarette smoking (more than 15/day) trebles the risk but heavier smokers have only a small further increase in risk. In the older men (aged 55–64, lower half of figure) the relative increase is rather less.

smokers at younger ages but only about one and a half times at older ages (Figure 6. 1). These increased risks are not so large as for lung cancer or bronchitis, but since the disease is so common the number of premature deaths from it that are associated with cigarette smoking is very large. In the four studies, between one third and one half of all the excess deaths in cigarette smokers were due to coronary heart disease. Although women are much less often affected than are men, cigarette smoking increases their risk similarly [18]. The evidence against cigarette smoking is supported by the greater mortality of those who inhale than of those who do not, and of those who begin smoking at early ages [18, 22].

6. 4　A number of surveys of large populations have shown that non-fatal attacks of coronary heart disease are more frequent in smokers of cigarettes than in non-smokers or pipe smokers, and that the incidence is parallel with the numbers of cigarettes smoked [8, 14, 17, 21, 23, 33, 36, 40, 41, 45, 56, 50].

6. 5　A recent report on prospective studies carried out over five years in seven countries showed the expected association between cigarette smoking and deaths from coronary heart disease in American men but no significant association among men in Italy, Finland, Slovenia, Serbia, Japan and Corfu, or Crete [26]. If this unexpected finding is confirmed it will not contradict the clear evidence of the association between coronary heart disease and cigarette smoking in North America and Britain but may provide an opportunity for discovering whether there is some special characteristic of cigarette smoking or cigarette smokers in these countries which enhances the risk of cigarette smoking and which, if avoided, might reduce it.

6. 6　*Smoking and angina pectoris* (*see* footnote, page 82). Most but not all these studies indicate that angina pectoris is commoner in cigarette smokers than in non-smokers. Tobacco smoking may bring on angina in some patients [35, 38]. Angina also occurs on less effort after smoking [1] presumably owing to the increased amount of work the heart is stimulated to perform through the action of nicotine, for this effect is reduced when low nicotine cigarettes are smoked [2]. The electrocardiogram taken during cigarette smoking may

undergo changes suggesting reduction in the blood supply of the heart [10, 27a, 42].

6. 7 *Smoking and abnormal coronary arteries.* In three large studies in the USA [4, 43, 47] and one in the USSR [3] the frequency and severity of atheroma (*see* footnote, page 82) of the coronary arteries observed at necropsy were found to have a consistent relationship with cigarette smoking. One survey in Chile reported a similar trend, but it was not statistically significant [54].

6. 8 *Other risk factors.* Coronary heart disease is common among non-smokers, and many factors other than smoking affect its incidence [50, 51, 52a]. These include high blood

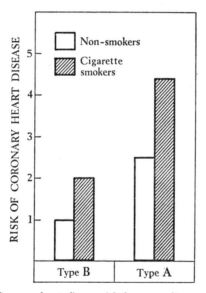

Figure 6. 2 *Coronary heart disease risk by personality type and smoking.* Type A men have a high degree of competitiveness, drive, aggression, and urgency in their work. Type B men have a more placid temperament. In both types cigarette smokers have a similarly increased risk of developing coronary heart disease compared with non-smokers of the same type; but both smokers and non-smokers of Type A have a greater risk than those of Type B. The scale indicates the number of times the risk in the other group is increased as compared with that of Type B non-smokers [51].

pressure, obesity, diabetes, raised levels of blood cholesterol,*
physical inactivity, impaired lung function, and type of personality. The effect of personality is illustrated in Figure 6. 2.
Men with a high degree of competitiveness, drive, aggressive-
ness, and urgency in their work (Type A) are more prone to
coronary heart disease than those with a more placid temperament (Type B), yet cigarette smokers in both groups
are about twice as prone as are non-smokers of the same
personality type [21, 41, 51]. The greater risk of cigarette
smokers might, it has been suggested, be due to their having
more of these characteristics than non-smokers. But it has
been shown that the effect of smoking is independent of these
factors when they are considered separately (Table 6. 1). To

TABLE 6. 1

*Effect of cigarette smoking on incidence of coronary heart disease in men
with and without other risk factors* [51]

Risk factor	Contrasting groups	Ratio of CHD incidence compared with non-smokers in lower risk group	
		Non-cigarette smokers	*Cigarette smokers*
Blood pressure (systolic)	Under 130 130 or more	1·0 1·8	2·1 3·8 (2·1)
Blood cholesterol	Low High	1·0 2·0	1·8 4·5 (2·3)
Physical activity	Most active Least active	1·0 2·4	2·6 3·4 (1·4)
Social mobility	Stable Mobile	1·0 2·3	1·5 3·2 (1·4)
Behaviour type	Type B Type A	1·0 2·5	2·0 4·4 (1·8)

This table is derived from various American studies [51]. It gives the age-
standardised incidence of coronary heart disease in men taking the incidence of
non-cigarette smokers in the lower risk group as 1·0. The figures in brackets
give the increased risk of cigarette smokers compared with non-cigarette
smokers in the higher risk groups.

* Cholesterol is a fatty constituent of the blood. It is in part the result of
chemical processes within the body but is also derived from foods rich in animal
fat, such as fat meat, cream, butter and cheese.

demonstrate the real independence of cigarette smoking it is necessary to use elaborate statistical techniques. Three such investigations have shown clearly the independent association of cigarette smoking with coronary heart disease [21, 33, 48]. It remains to decide whether this association is due to cause and effect.

6. 9   *Inheritance of smoking habits and coronary heart disease.* As in the case of lung cancer (para 4. 26) it has been suggested the extra risk of cigarette smokers may not be due to their smoking but to their inheriting both a desire to smoke cigarettes and a liability to coronary disease. In support of this suggestion it has been reported that in pairs of identical twins with differing smoking habits there is no association between angina pectoris and cigarette smoking [11, 12, 29]. The importance of this finding is uncertain for various technical reasons [52b]. The crucial question is whether deaths from coronary heart disease will be found to differ in twin pairs with different smoking habits, but the number of twins so far studied has been too small to provide an answer.

6. 10   *Effect of stopping smoking cigarettes.* If heredity were responsible for the increased risk of cigarette smokers this would be unaffected by giving up smoking. In fact the excess risk declines steadily after stopping. After ten years of abstinence the risk is close to that of non-smokers [7, 13a] although the risk to those who were heavier smokers continues to be raised [18, 22] (Figure 6. 3). The lower risk of those who have given up could possibly be due to their having inherited fewer adverse factors or having started smoking later or inhaled less than continuing smokers, but the steady decline of the extra risk makes these explanations unlikely.

6. 11   The experience of British doctors aged 35–64, many of whom have stopped smoking, compared with other men of the same ages, few of whom did so, confirms the benefits of stopping [13b]. Between 1953–57 and 1961–65 a 6 per cent fall in deaths from coronary heart disease was recorded in doctors while in all men in England and Wales there was apparently a 32 per cent increase. Over the same period an 18 per cent fall in mortality from other diseases of the heart and blood vessels in all men is to be compared with a 6 per

cent fall in doctors (Table 2. 3). It is therefore possible that part of the recorded increase of deaths from coronary heart disease in all men could have been due to increasing precision of diagnosis in the general public while there was no such change in doctors. A better comparison is therefore obtained if deaths from all diseases of the heart and blood vessels are considered together. It is then found that over this period there was a 6 per cent fall in deaths of doctors from these diseases compared with a 9 per cent rise in all men. Insurance statistics also confirm a favourable recent trend of coronary deaths among doctors [31].

6. 12   It may be concluded that even if inherited characteristics may make some people more prone to take up cigarette smoking and more liable to coronary heart disease the effects of this dangerous combination can be mitigated by avoidance of smoking.

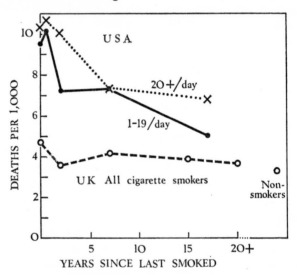

Figure 6. 3   The decline of death rates from coronary heart disease which follows stopping smoking cigarettes. In American men aged 30–79 the decline in coronary death rates is such that in the lighter smokers the risk has reached non-smoking levels after ten years, although the heavier smokers retain a higher risk. In the British doctors aged 35 and over the decline is more gradual and the risk is still above non-smoking levels after twenty or more years of abstinence.

6. 13   *Laboratory studies.* Experimental evidence of its effects on the blood and heart (para 3. 20) strengthens the conclusion that cigarette smoking enhances liability both to develop and to die from coronary heart disease. Recurrent rises in levels of cholesterol and other fats in the blood may result in increased atheroma in the coronary and other arteries of cigarette smokers. The greater likelihood of the blood to thrombose that is observed after cigarette smoking would be expected to raise the incidence of attacks of coronary thrombosis.

6. 14   Smoking has long been recognised as precipitating attacks of paroxysmal tachycardia,* and there is laboratory evidence that nicotine heightens liability to disturbances of the cardiac rhythm such as are commonly the cause of death after coronary thrombosis [6, 55]. The diminished oxygen content of the blood resulting from the action of carbon monoxide in cigarette smokers may also be dangerous to anyone with disease of the coronary arteries which has reduced the supply of blood to the heart.

6. 15   In normal men cigarette smoking increases the output of blood from the heart and the flow of blood in the coronary arteries. In men who have had a coronary thrombosis, however, the output of the heart and the coronary artery flow may not respond normally to exercise after smoking, indicating a potentially serious impairment of heart function [37, 39].

6. 16   *Coronary heart disease in smokers of pipes or cigars.* Most of the large surveys have shown little if any greater danger of coronary heart disease in smokers of pipes or cigars. They are mostly light smokers, but those who smoke heavily or who inhale run an increased risk but not as large as that of light cigarette smokers [18]. There is little evidence about absorption of nicotine from pipe or cigar smoke or of the immediate effects of such smoke on the heart and blood vessels but the effect on blood fat levels after pipe or cigar smoking is less than after cigarette smoking so long as the smoke is not inhaled [25].

---

* This is a bout of rapid and often irregular beating of the heart, which may cause unpleasant sensations of palpitation or breathlessness and if prolonged may result in heart failure.

6. 17   *Conclusion.* In Britain, cigarette smoking is an important factor in causing disease of the coronary arteries—one of the principal causes of death. In the absence of cigarette smoking the death rate from this disease between the ages of 35 and 64 might well be reduced by as much as 25 per cent in men and 20 per cent in women representing in England and Wales a saving each year of the lives of some 7,000 men and 1,500 women at these ages.

Smoking and Other Arterial Diseases

6. 18   Although the immediate action of nicotine is to raise the blood pressure there is no evidence that smoking causes sustained high blood pressure [16, 24]. Indeed, surveys have shown that the average blood pressure of cigarette smokers tends to be slightly lower than that in non-smokers, pipe smokers having intermediate levels. The small differences may be due in part to the smokers being leaner, and are unlikely to be of any importance to health.

6. 19   It has long been considered that cigarette smoking is an important factor in the development of atherosclerotic disease of arteries throughout the body, reducing the flow of blood to the affected parts, for the disease is commoner in smokers than in non-smokers [27b]. The arteries of the legs are most often attacked, with pain that comes on when the muscles require more blood during walking ('intermittent claudication'); eventually gangrene may necessitate amputation of the limb. Recent evidence has confirmed the adverse effect of smoking [5, 15, 28, 34] on blood vessels. Thromboangiitis obliterans, a rare form of arterial disease, hardly ever occurs in non-smokers and continuing smoking makes it worse [27b, 30].

6. 20   The largest American prospective surveys have also disclosed an increased liability to strokes in both male and female cigarette smokers, death rates from strokes rising with increasing cigarette smoking at all ages up to 75 [19, 22]. In heavy cigarette smokers the death rate exceeded that of non-smokers by some 70 per cent. Pipe and cigar smokers had the same rates as non-smokers. The survey of British doctors did not, however, reveal a heightened risk from arterial disease

other than coronary heart disease among cigarette smokers
[13*a*].

REFERENCES

1. Aronow, W. S., Kaplan, M. A., and Jacob, D. (1968). 'Tobacco: a precipitating factor in angina pectoris.' *Ann. intern. Med.*, **69**, 529.

2. Aronow, W. S., and Swanson, A. J. (1969). 'The effect of low nicotine cigarettes on angina pectoris.' *Ann. intern. Med.*, **71**, 599.

3. Avtandilov, G. G., Kolenova, V. I., and Ponomarenko, C. V. (1965). 'Tobacco smoking and the degree of atherosclerotic lesions of the coronary arteries of the heart and aorta.' *Kardiologiya*, **5**, 30.

4. Auerbach, O., Hammond, E. C., and Garfinkel, L. (1965). 'Smoking in relation to atherosclerosis of the coronary arteries.' *New Engl. J. Med.*, **273**, 775.

5. Begg, T. B. (1965). 'Characteristics of men with intermittent claudication.' *Practitioner*, **194**, 202.

6. Bellet, S., Kershbaum, A., Meade, R. H., and Schwartz, L. (1941). 'The effect of tobacco smoke and nicotine on the normal heart and in the presence of myocardial damage produced by coronary ligation.' *Amer. J. med. Sci.*, **201**, 40.

7. Best, E. W. R. (1966). *A Canadian Study of Smoking and Health.* Department of National Health and Welfare, Ottawa.

8. Borhani, N. O., Hechter, H. H., and Breslow, L. (1963). 'Report of a ten-year follow-up study of the San Francisco longshore men. Mortality from coronary heart disease and from all causes.' *J. chron. Dis.*, **16**, 1251.

9. Bronte-Stewart, B., Keys, A., and Brock, J. F. (1955). 'Serum-cholesterol, diet and coronary heart disease.' *Lancet*, **2**, 1103.

10. Buxtorf, J. C., and Beaumont, J. L. (1968). 'Tabac et électro-cardiogramme.' *Path. Biol., Paris*, **16**, 877.

11. Cederlof, R., Friberg, L., and Hrubec, Z. (1969). 'Cardiovascular and respiratory symptoms in relation to tobacco smoking. A study of American twins.' *Archs. envir. Hlth.*, **18**, 934.

12. Cederlof, R., Friberg, L., and Jonsson, E. (1967). 'Hereditary factors and "angina pectoris".' A study on 5,877 twin-pairs with the aid of mailed questionnaires. *Archs. environ. Hlth.*, **14**, 397.

13*a*. Doll, R., and Hill, A. B. (1964). 'Mortality in relation to smoking: Ten years' observation of British doctors.' *Brit. med. J.*, **1**, 1399, 1460.

13*b*. Doll, R., and Pike, M. C. (1970). Unpublished data.

14. Doyle, J. T., Dawber, T. R., Kannel, W. B., Kinch, S. H., and Kahn, H. A. (1964). 'The relationship of cigarette smoking to coronary heart disease.' *J. Amer. med. Ass.*, **190**, 886.

15. Eastcott, H. H. (1962). 'Rarity of lower-limb ischaemia in non-smokers.' *Lancet*, **2**, 1117.

16. Edwards, F., McKeown, T., and Whitfield, A. G. W. (1959). 'Association between smoking and disease in men over sixty.' *Lancet*, **1**, 196.

17. EPSTEIN, F. H., OSTRANDER, L. D., JOHNSON, B. C., PAYNE, M. W., HAYNER, N. S., KELLER, J. B., and FRANCIS, T. (1965). 'Epidemiological studies of cardiovascular disease in a total community—Tecumseh, Michigan.' *Ann. intern. Med.*, **62**, 1170.

18. HAMMOND, E. C. (1966). 'Smoking in relation to the death rates of one million men and women.' *Natn. Cancer Inst. Monogr.*, **19**, 127.

19. HAMMOND, E. C., and GARFINKEL, L. (1969). 'Coronary heart disease, stroke and aortic aneurysm. Factors in the etiology.' *Archs. envir. Hlth.*, **19**, 167.

20. HERRICK, J. B. (1912). 'Clinical features of sudden obstruction of the coronary arteries.' *J. Am. med. Ass.*, **59**, 2015.

21. JENKINS, C. D., ROSENMAN, R. H., and ZYZANSKI, S. J. (1968). 'Cigarette smoking. Its relationship to coronary heart disease and related risk factors in the Western Collaborative Group Study.' *Circulation*, **38**, 1140.

22. KAHN, H. A. (1966). 'The Dorn Study of smoking and mortality among US veterans. Report on eight and a half years of observation.' *Natn. Cancer Inst. Monogr.*, **19**, 1.

23. KANNEL, W. B., CASTELLI, W. P., and McNAMARA, P. M. (1968). 'Cigarette smoking and risk of coronary heart disease. Epidemiological clues to pathogenesis. The Framingham study.' *Natn. Cancer Inst. Monogr.*, **28**, 9.

24. KARVONEN, M., ORMA, E., KEYS, A., FIDANZA, F., and BROZEK, J. (1959). 'Cigarette smoking, serum-cholesterol, blood pressure and body fatness.' *Lancet*, **1**, 492.

25. KERSHBAUM, A., and BELLET, S. (1968). 'Cigarette, cigar and pipe smoking. Some differences in biochemical effects.' *Geriatrics*, **23**, 126.

26. KEYS, A. (1970). 'Coronary heart disease in seven countries.' *Circulation*, **41**, Suppl. 1.

27. LARSON, P. S., HAAG, H. B., SILVETTE, H. (1961). *Tobacco: experimental and clinical Studies.* A comprehensive account of the world literature. The Williams Wilkins Co., Baltimore. *a*, p. 203; *b*, p. 677.

28. LARSON, P. H., and SILVETTE, H. (1968). *Tobacco: experimental and clinical Studies.* Suppl. 1. The William Wilkins Co., Baltimore, p. 468.

29. LUNDMAN, T. (1966). 'Smoking in relation to coronary heart disease and lung function in twins. A co-twin control study.' *Acta med. scand.*, **180**, Suppl. 455, 1–75.

30. McPHERSON, J. R., JUERGENS and GIFFORD, R. W. (1963). 'Thromboangiitis obliterans and arteriosclerosis obliterans: clinical and prognostic differences.' *Ann. intern. Med.*, **59**, 288.

31. MEADE, T. W., ARIE, T. H. D., BREWIS, M., BOND, D. J., and MORRIS, J. N. (1968). 'Recent history of ischaemic heart disease and duodenal ulcer in doctors.' *Br. med. J.*, **3**, 701.

32. MORRIS, J. N. (1951). 'Recent history of coronary disease.' *Lancet*, **1**, 1 and 69.

33. MORRIS, J. N., KAGAN, A. PATTISON, D. C., GARDNER, M. J., and RAFFLE, P. A. B. (1966). 'Incidence and prediction of ischaemic heart disease in London busmen.' *Lancet*, **2**, 553.

34. OLDHAM, J. B. (1964). 'Claudication: the case for conservatism.' *J. R. Coll. Surg. Edinb.*, **9**, 179.

35. ORAM, S., and SOWTON, E. (1963). 'Tobacco angina.' *Q., J. Med.*, **32**, 115.

36. PAUL, O., LEPPER, M. H., PHELAN, W. H., DUPERTUIS, G. W., MACMILLAN, A., McKEAN, H., and PARK, H. (1963). 'A longitudinal study of coronary heart disease.' *Circulation*, **28**, 20.

37. PENTECOST, B., and SHILLINGFORD, J. (1964). 'The acute effects of smoking on myocardial performance in patients with coronary arterial disease.' *Br. Heart J.*, **26**, 422.

38. PICKERING, G. W., and SANDERSON, P. H. (1945). 'Angina pectoris and tobacco.' *Clin. Sci.*, **5**, 275.

39. REGAN, T. J., FRANK, M. J., McGINTY, J. F., ZOBL, E., HELLEMS, H. K., and BING, R. J. (1961). 'Myocardial response to cigarette smoking in normal subjects and patients with coronary disease.' *Circulation*, **23**, 365.

40. REID, D. D., CORNFIELD, J., MARKUSH, R. E., SEIGEL, D., PEDERSEN, E., and HAENSZEL, W. (1966). 'Studies of disease among migrants and native populations in Great Britain, Norway and the United States. III Prevalence of cardiorespiratory symptoms among migrants and native born in the United States.' *Natn. Cancer Inst. Monogr.*, **19**, 321.

41. ROSENMAN, R. H., FRIEDMAN, M., STRAUS, R., WURM, M., KOSITCHEK, R., HAHN, W., and WERTHESSEN, N. T. (1964). 'A predictive study of coronary heart disease.' *J. Am. med. Ass.*, **189**, 15.

42. ROTH, G. M., and SHICK, R. M. (1958). 'Effect of smoking on the cardiovascular system of man.' *Circulation*, **17**, 443.

43. SACKETT, D. L., GIBSON, R. W., BROSS, I. D. J., and PICKREN, J. W. (1968). 'Relation between aortic atherosclerosis and the use of cigarettes and alcohol: an autopsy study.' *New Engl. J. Med.*, **279**, 1413.

44. SELTZER, C. C. (1968). 'An evaluation of the effect of smoking on coronary heart disease. I. Epidemiological evidence.' *J. Am. med. Ass.*, **203**, 193.

45. SHAPIRO, S., WEINBLATT, E., FRANK, C. W., and SAGER, R. V. (1969). 'Incidence of coronary heart disease in a population insured for medical care (HIP). Myocardial infarction, angina pectoris, and possible myocardial infarction.' *Am. J. publ. Hlth.*, **59**, Suppl.

46. STAMLER, J., BERKSON, D. M., LEVINSON, M. J., MOJONNIER, L., EPSTEIN, M. B., HALL, Y., BURKEY, F., SOYUGENC, R., and ANDELMAN, S. L. (1968). 'A long-term coronary prevention evaluation program.' *Ann. N.Y. Acad. Sci.*, **149**, 1022.

47. STRONG, J. P., McGILL, H. C., RICHARDS, M. L., and EGGEN, D. A. (1966). 'Relationship between cigarette smoking habits and coronary atherosclerosis in autopsied males.' *Circulation*, **33–34**, Suppl. 3.

48. TRUETT, J., CORNFIELD, J., and KANNEL, W. (1967). 'A multivariate analysis of the risk of coronary heart disease in Framingham.' *J. chron. Dis.*, **20**, 511.

49. US PUBLIC HEALTH SERVICE. SURGEON GENERAL'S ADVISORY COMMITTEE ON SMOKING AND HEALTH (1964). *Smoking and Health*. Public Health Service Publication No. 1103, p. 326.

50. US PUBLIC HEALTH SERVICE (1966). *The Framingham Heart Study*. US Public Health Service Publ. No. 1515.

51. US PUBLIC HEALTH SERVICE (1967). *The Health Consequences of Smoking*. A Public Service Health Review. Public Health Service Publication No. 1696, pp. 55–57.

52. US PUBLIC HEALTH SERVICE (1968). Supplement to Public Health Service Publication No. 1696 on the *Health Consequences of Smoking. a*, p. 21; *b*, p. 29.

53. US PUBLIC HEALTH SERVICE (1969). Supplement to Public Health Service Publication No. 1969 on the *Health Consequences of Smoking*, pp. 16–20.

54. VIEL, B., DONOSO, S., and SALCEDO, D. (1968). 'Coronary atherosclerosis in persons dying violently.' *Arch. intern. Med.*, **122,** 97.

55. WEBB, W. R., WAX, S. D., SUGG, W. L. (1968). 'Cigarette smoke and fibrillation threshold in dogs.' *Clin. Res.*, **16,** 74.

7 *Smoking and Other Conditions*

Pregnancy

7. 1   There is now no doubt that a mother who smokes during pregnancy may by so doing retard the growth of her unborn child [1, 12, 23, 43, 46, 52, 53, 58, 62*b*, 67]. The babies born to women who smoke weigh on average, 5 to 8 ounces (150 to 240 gm) less than those of mothers who do not, and mothers who smoke have two or three times as many premature babies (defined as those weighing less than $5\frac{1}{2}$ lb or 2·5 kg at birth). The smallness of these babies cannot be explained by other influences on their weights, such as mother's age, height, social class, education, number of previous pregnancies, or attitudes to pregnancy [1, 12, 46, 52]. Heavier smokers are more likely than lighter smokers to have small babies. By their first birthdays the smokers' babies have, on average, caught up and are as heavy as those of the non-smoking mothers [53]; this suggests that their development has been freed from a delaying influence.

7. 2   It is not known how smoking during pregnancy retards the baby's growth. This retardation is not due to the mother's eating habits since smoking and non-smoking pregnant women gain weight at the same rate [52, 58, 62*b*]. It has been suggested that smoking may restrict the blood flow to the placenta and so reduce the amount of nourishment which the baby receives [43]. Carbon monoxide in the blood of a smoking mother, transferred to the baby's circulation, may also be harmful [28, 66].

7. 3   Recent investigations in the United Kingdom, Ireland, and other countries have shown ways in which a mother may endanger her baby by smoking. In several large studies it has

been found that mothers who smoked during pregnancy were more likely to have a miscarriage, to have a still-born baby, or one which died soon after birth [12, 46, 52]. This loss of young life was independent of social and constitutional influences. In the prospective study in Sheffield [53], which involved over 2,000 pregnancies, 7·9 per cent of mothers who smoked during their pregnancy lost their babies compared with 4·1 per cent of those who did not smoke. One in five of the smoking mothers who lost their babies might not have done so if they had not smoked [53a]. In other surveys no significant effect of smoking on the infants' survival has been found [58, 65].

7. 4 The babies of mothers with pre-eclamptic toxaemia (raised blood pressure and protein in the urine) are always in more danger than those of mothers without this condition. Although mothers who smoke tend to have a lower blood pressure and are less liable to toxaemia than non-smokers, the risk to the baby, if this does occur, has been found to be so much higher in smokers that the total risk to their babies is increased [23].

7. 5 There is no doubt that smoking during pregnancy retards the unborn baby's growth. Although there is conflicting evidence about whether or not smoking also increases the risk of abortion, stillbirth and death to the baby after delivery [62b], recent reports certainly suggest that women who abstain from smoking when they are pregnant do more than protect their own health.

Cancer of Various Organs

7. 6 An association of cancers of the mouth, pharynx, larynx, and the oesophagus with smoking of cigarettes or of pipes and cigars has been shown by several investigations [21a, 30, 34, 59a, 60a], and pre-cancerous changes in the larynx and oesophagus have been observed more often in men who had smoked than in non-smokers [5, 62a]. In Dorn's prospective study of American veterans mortality from these cancers was directly related to the number of cigarettes smoked [34]; since, however, in respect of cancer of the mouth and larynx there is also an association with heavy

drinking [63, 64], alcohol may also contribute to their causation. Although these cancers are not uncommon they are often curable and make a small contribution to the excess mortality of cigarette smokers compared with non-smokers.

7.7 Cancer of the bladder has become more frequent in Great Britain [14, 51], in America [61] and in Denmark [15] in men more than in women. Several retrospective studies have indicated that cigarette smokers have approximately twice the risk of non-smokers from this disease [20, 59b, 60b]. In Denmark a clearer association was shown when bladder papillomata,* which may precede bladder cancer, were included [41]. Large prospective studies in America [30, 34] and Canada [7] have confirmed this heightened risk, which is related to increasing cigarette consumption and is lower in pipe and cigar smokers. In the first ten years of the study of British doctors no association of smoking with the small numbers of deaths from bladder cancer could be detected [21a] but after fifteen years a slight association was observed [21b].

7.8 It is difficult to see how bladder cancer could be causally related to smoking but it is known to be induced by industrial exposure, presumably by inhalation, to certain chemicals (aromatic amines) [8, 13, 14]. A hint of a possible mechanism has been given by one small study [37]. Certain carcinogenic substances are normally present in the urine in very small amounts as a result of the breakdown of the amino-acid tryptophan. They were found in greater amounts than normal in the urine of three cigarette smokers and decreased when they stopped smoking, and also increased in amount in the urine of three non-smokers when they started smoking.

7.9 The only other cancer known to be associated with smoking is that of the pancreas, as shown by prospective studies in America [30, 34], Canada [7], and Japan [32]; but this adds little to the total excess deaths of smokers.

Gastric and Duodenal Ulcers (Peptic Ulcers)

7.10 That smoking affects the stomach and intestines is

* Wart-like growths in the lining of the bladder.

within the experience of most smokers. Apart from the nausea and vomiting after the first smoke, perhaps the best known effect on the digestive system of established smokers is relief of hunger. A few puffs of a cigarette can inhibit hunger contractions of the stomach. The usual rise in weight after giving up smoking [11] and the fact that non-smokers are on average a little heavier than smokers may not, however, be simply due to their eating more (para 7. 24).

7. 11   In studies of the effects of nicotine on the normal human stomach a reduction of gastric activity has usually but not always been observed. Patients with peptic ulcers have similar patterns of response after smoking one cigarette, but two cigarettes are more likely to increase activity and pain [17]. Some patients with peptic ulcer secrete more acid after smoking, in others the effect is small.

7. 12   A clear association between smoking and peptic ulcer is evident from retrospective studies [59c]. Patients with gastric or duodenal ulcer are more often smokers and tend to be heavier smokers than patients with other diseases. In two large surveys, one of men over 60 in Britain [24] and one of men and women in the USA [29], there were more people with peptic ulcer among cigarette smokers than among non-smokers, and more in heavy than light smokers.

7. 13   Patients often report that heavy smoking makes indigestion worse; this could be because stress both causes them to smoke more and aggravates their pain. In 300 smokers, various symptoms of indigestion improved in most of them when they stopped smoking [27]. In an investigation [6] of the effect of smoking on the medical management of ulcers in 108 patients, it was shown that those who continued to smoke responded less well to treatment and had more frequent relapses than those who ceased.

7. 14   A controlled trial in Britain demonstrated the effect of smoking on the rate of healing of gastric ulcers, whose size, unlike that of duodenal ulcers, can be measured accurately [22]. Hospital patients with gastric ulcer were divided into two groups, all being smokers; the first group were advised not to smoke and the second were not. Both had the same

four weeks' medical treatment in bed. Among forty patients advised to give up smoking, most of whom did so, the average reduction in the size of the ulcer was 78 per cent compared with 57 per cent for those not so advised and who continued smoking. The difference was significant, and it was concluded that smoking interferes with healing, thus encouraging chronic ulceration. In some of the patients who continued to smoke the ulcer actually grew in size—a deterioration not seen in any of those who discontinued.

7. 15 *Deaths from peptic ulcer.* According to prospective studies death rates from peptic ulcer [21a, 30, 34] are higher in smokers than in non-smokers, and higher in cigarette smokers than in pipe or cigar smokers or ex-smokers. In the large survey of American veterans, where it was possible to

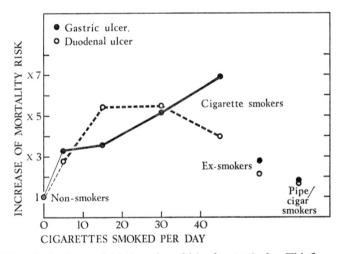

Figure 7. 1 *Increased risks in smokers of dying from peptic ulcer.* This figure, derived from Dorn's prospective study of American veterans [34], shows the increased risk of dying from duodenal and gastric ulcers in various groups of smokers and ex-smokers compared with non-smokers. The increase of risk tends to be higher for gastric than for duodenal ulcer, and is related to the number of cigarettes smoked. The lower risk of duodenal ulcer in the heaviest cigarette smokers may be due to some of those with the most severe symptoms having cut their smoking before the beginning of the study. Pipe and cigar smokers and ex-smokers have only a small increase of risk.

separate gastric and duodenal ulcers (Figure 7. 1), the rates
were similar in moderate and in heavy smokers. The concentration of deaths among moderate smokers observed in
other studies may be due to reduction in the amount smoked
by heavy smokers with severe symptoms. The relationship
between smoking and peptic ulcer is closer for gastric than
for duodenal ulcer. The excess liability to bronchitis in
cigarette smokers, could increase their liability to die from
complications of peptic ulcer, but associated respiratory
disease would be unlikely to account for the greater frequency of peptic ulcers in cigarette smokers during life.

7. 16.   Peptic ulcers commonly affect non-smokers and the
incidence of gastric ulcers has fallen during the many years
in which tobacco consumption in the United Kingdom has
been rising; duodenal ulcers have become more prevalent.
But the world-wide distribution of mortality from duodenal
ulcer is quite unlike that of tobacco smoking. Smoking does
not directly cause ulcers in the stomach and duodenum,
but the evidence that it delays healing of established ulcers
provides a simple explanation for both the increased prevalence of peptic ulcer and of the increased risk of death among
cigarette smokers; for delay in healing increases the risk of
serious complications such as haemorrhage or perforation.

Tuberculosis of the Lungs

7. 17   The number of deaths from pulmonary tuberculosis in
Britain declined steadily in both men and women throughout
the earlier part of this century, while cigarette smoking was
rapidly increasing among men and, later, among women.
When effective anti-tuberculosis drugs were introduced the
number of deaths fell more steeply (Figure 4. 1). Nevertheless, there is evidence that cigarette smokers are more
likely to suffer from pulmonary tuberculosis than are non-
smokers. Two surveys based on mass radiography [3, 42]
have shown a direct relationship between pulmonary
tuberculosis and cigarette smoking, and an association of
cigarette smoking with deaths from tuberculosis was found in
surveys of both British doctors [21a] and US veterans [34].
Moreover, changes over the past forty years in the relative

death rates of men and women from tuberculosis of the lung in Britain have resembled those for lung cancer and bronchitis, which are consistent with an effect of cigarette smoking [18]. Since the highest death rates from tuberculosis are among middle-aged and old men, who were probably first infected early in their lives, smoking may encourage the recrudescence of old tuberculous infection. Other studies have, however, suggested that the association between smoking and tuberculosis may be due to the higher alcohol consumption of smokers rather than to cigarette smoking itself [10, 38]. Present evidence does no more than indicate that cigarette smoking may increase the risk of breakdown of inactive tuberculosis in the lungs.

Accidents

7. 18 The most important accidental consequence of smoking is fires. In two investigations in the USA of deaths in fires 16 per cent and 18 per cent respectively had resulted from fires caused by smokers [59e, 60e]. The average annual number of deaths in fires in England and Wales from 1962–1967 was 792, so that if the American experience is applied to this country over 100 deaths would have resulted from fires caused by smoking each year during this period. One survey of industrial injuries disclosed that younger smokers were injured more frequently than non-smokers [44, 60e]. Several studies have indicated an association between traffic accidents and smoking [60e] but the evidence is inconclusive [33]. If smokers are more accident prone than non-smokers, this proneness could be due to differences in personality (para 8. 12) rather than to smoking habits.

Blindness

7. 19 Tobacco amblyopia attributed to heavy smoking, particularly of pipes and cigars, is a rare cause of blindness, long thought to be due to a combination between smoking and a nutritional deficiency [60c]. Recent evidence has suggested that damage to the optic nerves may result from the combined toxic action of cyanides absorbed from tobacco smoke (para 3. 2) and co-existent vitamin B_{12} deficiency

[31, 55]. Cyanides from the smoke may also be related to another rare form of optic atrophy [2].

7. 20   A decrease in night vision in smokers might be related to an increase of carbon monoxide levels in the blood. Since no effect of smoking on performance under simulated night driving conditions was found in a group of young drivers [33], this effect is unlikely to be important.

Cirrhosis of the Liver

7. 21   Deaths from cirrhosis of the liver are more frequent in cigarette smokers than in non-smokers [21a, 30, 34], but this is probably because heavy drinking, which is an important cause of this disease, is usually associated with heavy smoking [59d, 60d].

Diseases of the Teeth and Gums

7. 22   During the past twenty years many studies have shown that smokers are more liable than non-smokers to a variety of inflammatory conditions of the gums [62c]. The association of gingivitis with smoking [56] may be because smokers tend to have lower standards of oral hygiene [9]. Service recruits who smoke are liable to acute infective conditions of the mouth including, for instance, Vincent's gingivitis [45]. In one Danish study the frequency of these conditions was found to rise with increasing tobacco consumption [50]. Pipe smokers are as often affected as cigarette smokers. The association between diseases of the gums and smoking may account for the finding in two surveys that smokers have more often had all their teeth extracted than non-smokers [57].

Body Weight

7. 23   Comparison of the weights in surveys of working men have shown that the non-smokers tend to be slightly heavier and taller than smokers, but in students the differences are not consistent [4, 19, 36, 40, 47, 48, 54].

7. 24   Smokers who stop often find they gain weight and the gain may be considerable [11]. British doctors who ceased smoking gained, on average, four pounds [25]. They

had to take more care with their diet than those who continued to smoke and after ten years were only one pound heavier than before they had stopped. The gain in weight is usually attributed to the greater appetite which many smokers report on stopping smoking. Recently, however, it has been noted that although cigarette smokers are on average lighter than non-smokers they eat more [39]. Metabolic changes occur when they stop smoking which might explain a gain in weight despite reduced intake of food. These changes include reduced oxygen consumption and reduced blood glucose [26].

7. 25 It has been suggested that the gain in weight on ceasing to smoke might increase the risk of coronary heart disease more than the risk is reduced by smoking itself. That this is untrue is shown by the steady decrease in the cigarette smokers' excess risk of coronary heart disease after smoking is given up (para 6. 10).

Physical Fitness

7. 26 That smoking is 'bad for the wind' is widely admitted by smokers and this is why few serious athletes smoke during training. Until recently there was little scientific basis for this popular belief; obvious adverse effects of smoking appeared only in middle-aged or older people. Now, however, there is clear evidence that cigarette smoking can impair the capacity of young people for strenuous exercise, and abstinence improves performance. In five out of thirteen students the time taken to complete a stint of vigorous bicycling was significantly improved by stopping smoking [35]. In an investigation of American airmen, endurance, maximum exercise capacity, and improvement on training were impaired in proportion to the number of cigarettes smoked daily and the duration of smoking [16]. Another study of young men showed that the maximum exercise capacity was lower and the improvement on training less in smokers than in non-smokers [49]. These observations are to be expected in view of the impairment of lung function caused by smoking (para 5. 5) and interference with the transport of oxygen to the tissues by the carbon monoxide in the blood of smokers (para 3. 23).

REFERENCES

1. ABERNATHY, J. R., GREENBERG, B. G., WELLS. H. B., and FRAZIER, T. M. (1966). 'Smoking as an independent variable in a multiple regression analysis upon birth weight and gestation.' *Am. J. publ. Hlth.*, **56**, 626.

2. ADAMS, J. H., BLACKWOOD, W., and WILSON, J. (1966). 'Further clinical and pathological observations on Leber's optic atrophy.' *Brain*, **89**, 15.

3. ADELSTEIN, A. M., and RIMINGTON, J. (1967). 'Smoking and pulmonary tuberculosis: an analysis based on a study of volunteers for mass miniature radiography.' *Tubercle, Lond.*, **48**, 219.

4. ASHFORD, J. R., BROWN, S., DUFFIELD, D. P., SMITH, C. S., and FAY, J. W. J. (1961). 'The relation between smoking habits and physique, respiratory symptoms, ventilatory function and radiologic pneumoconiosis amongst coal workers at three Scottish collieries.' *Br. J. prev. soc. Med.*, **15**, 106.

5. AUERBACH, O., STOUT, A. P., HAMMOND, E. C., and GARFINKEL, L. (1965). 'Histologic changes in esophagus in relation to smoking habits.' *Archs. envir. Hlth.*, **11**, 4.

6. BATTERMAN, R. C. (1955). 'The gastro-intestinal tract' in *The Biologic Effects of Tobacco*. Edit. by E. L. Wynder. Little, Brown & Co., Boston, p. 133.

7. BEST, E. W. R. (1966). *A Canadian Study of Smoking and Health*. Ottawa Dept. of National Health and Welfare.

8. BOYLAND, E. (1963). *The Biochemistry of Bladder Cancer*. C. C. Thomas, Illinois.

9. BRANDTZAEG, P., and JAMISON, H. C. (1964). 'A study of periodontal health and oral hygiene in Norwegian army recruits.' *J. Periodont*, **35**, 302.

10. BROWN, K. E., and CAMPBELL, A. H. (1961). 'Tobacco, alcohol and tuberculosis.' *Br. J. dis. Chest*, **55**, 150.

11. BROZEK, J., and KEYS, A. (1957). 'Changes of body weight in normal men who stop smoking cigarettes.' *Science, N.Y.*, **125**, 1203.

12. BUTLER, N., and ALBERMAN, E. D., ed. (1969). Perinatal Problems: *The Second Report of the British Perinatal Mortality Survey*, Edin., E. & S. Livingstone.

13. CASE, R. A. M., and HOSKER, M. E (1954). 'Tumour of the urinary bladder as an occupational disease in the rubber industry in England and Wales.' *Br. J. prev. soc. Med.*, **8**, 39.

14. CASE, R. A. M., HOSKER, M. E., McDONALD, D. B., and PEARSON, J. T. (1954). 'Tumours of urinary bladder in workmen engaged in the manufacture and use of certain dyestuff intermediates in British chemical industry.' *Br. J. ind. Med.*, **11**, 75.

15. CLEMMESEN, J. (1965). *Statistical Studies in the Aetiology of Malignant Neoplasms*. E. Munksgaard, Copenhagen, p. 358.

16. COOPER, K. H., GREY, G. O., and BOTTENBERG, R. A. (1968). 'Effects of cigarette smoking on endurance performance.' *J. Am. med. Ass.*, **203**, 189.

17. COOPER, P., HARROWER, H. W., STEIN, H. L., and MOORE, G. F. (1958). 'The effect of cigarette smoking on intragastric balloon pressure and temperature of patients with duodenal ulcer.' *Gastroenterology*, **35**, 176.

18. CROFTON, E., and CROFTON, J. (1963). 'Influence of smoking on mortality from various diseases in Scotland and in England and Wales.' *Br. med. J.*, **2**, 1161.

19. DAMON, A. (1962). 'Constitution and smoking in Italian-American factory workers.' *Am. J. phys. Anthrop.*, **20**, 67.

20. DEELEY, T. J., and COHEN, S. L. (1966). *The Relationship Between Cancer of the Bladder and Smoking.* Proceedings of 5th Inter-American Conference on Toxicology and Occupational Medicine, University of Miami, School of Medicine, Coral Sable, Florida, p. 163.

21a. DOLL, R., and HILL, A. B. (1964). 'Mortality in relation to smoking: ten years observations of British doctors.' *Br. med. J.*, **1**, 1460.

21b. DOLL, R., and PIKE, M. C. (1970). Personal communication.

22. DOLL, W. R., JONES, F. A., and PYGOTT, F. (1958). 'Effect of smoking on the production and maintenance of gastric and duodenal ulcers.' *Lancet*, **1**, 657.

23. DUFFUS, G. M., and MACGILLIVRAY, I. (1968). 'The incidence of pre-eclamptic toxaemia in smokers and non-smokers.' *Lancet*, **1**, 994.

24. EDWARDS, F., McKEOWN, T., and WHITFIELD, A. G. W. (1959). 'Association between smoking and disease in men over sixty.' *Lancet*, **1**, 196.

25. FLETCHER, C., and DOLL, R. (1969). 'A survey of doctors' attitudes to smoking.' *Br. J. prev. soc. Med.*, **23**, 145.

26. GLAUSER, S. C., GLAUSER, E. M., REIDENBERG, M. M., RUSY, B. F., and TALLARIDA, R. J. (1970). 'Metabolic changes associated with the cessation of cigarette smoking.' *Archs. envir. Hlth.*, **20**, 377.

27. GRAY, I. (1929). 'Tobacco smoking and gastric symptoms.' *Ann. intern. Med.*, **3**, 267.

28. HADDON, W., NESBITT, R. E. L., and GARCIA, R. (1961). 'Smoking and pregnancy: carbon monoxide in blood during gestation and at term.' *Obstet. and Gynec.*, *N.Y.*, **18**, 262.

29. HAMMOND, E. C. (1964). 'Smoking in relation to mortality and morbidity.' *J. natn. Cancer Inst.*, **32**, 1161.

30. HAMMOND, E. C. (1966). 'Smoking in relation to death rates of one million men and women.' *Natn. Cancer Inst. Monogr.*, **19**, 127.

31. HEATON, J. M., McCORMICK, A. J. A., and FREEMAN, A. G. (1958). 'Tobacco amblyopia: a clinical manifestation of Vitamin B_{12} deficiency.' *Lancet*, **2**, 286.

32. HIRAYAMA, T. (1967). *Smoking in Relation to the death rates of 265,118 men and women in Japan.* Tokyo National Cancer Centre, Research Institute, Epidemiology Division, Sept., 1967.

33. JOHANSSON, G., and JANSSON, G. (1965). 'Smoking and night driving.' *Scand. J. Psychol.*, **6**, 124.

34. KAHN, H. A. (1966). 'The Dorn study of smoking and mortality among US veterans: Report on eight and one-half years of observation.' *Natn. Cancer Inst. Monogr.*, **19**, 1.

35. KARPOVITCH, P. V., and HALE, C. J. (1951). 'Tobacco smoking and physical performance.' *J. appl. Physiol.*, **3**, 616.

36. KARVONEN, M., ORMA, E., KEYS, A., FIDANZA, F., and BROZEK, J. (1959). 'Cigarette smoking, serum cholesterol, blood pressure and body fatness.' *Lancet*, **1**, 492.

37. KERR, W. K., BARKIN, M., LEVERS, P. E., WOO, S. K. C., and MENCZYK, Z. (1965). 'The effect of cigarette smoking on bladder carcinogens in man.' *Can. med. Ass. J.*, **93**, 1.

38. LEWIS, J. G., and CHAMBERLAIN, D. A. (1963). 'Alcohol consumption and smoking habits in male patients with pulmonary tuberculosis.' *Br. J. prev. soc. Med.*, **17** 149.

39. LINCOLN, J. E. (1969). 'Weight gain after cessation of smoking.' *J. Am. med. Ass.*, **210**, 1765.

40. LIVSON, N., and STEWART, L. H. (1965). 'Morphological constitution and smoking. A further evaluation.' *J. Am. med. Ass.*, **192**, 806.

41. LOCKWOOD, K. (1961). 'On the etiology of bladder tumours in Kobenhaven-Frederiskberg.' *Acta path. microbiol. scand.* **51.** suppl. 145, 41.

42. LOWE, C. R. (1956). 'An association between smoking and respiratory tuberculosis.' *Br. med. J.*, **2**, 1081.

43. LOWE, C. R. (1959). 'Effect of mothers' smoking habits on birth weight of their children.' *Br. med. J.*, **2**, 673.

44. LOWE, C. R. (1960). 'Smoking habits related to injury and absenteeism in industry.' *Br. J. prev. soc. Med.*, **14**, 57.

45. LUDWICK, W., and MASSLER, M. (1952). 'Relation of dental caries experience and gingivitis to cigarette smoking in males 17 to 21 years old.' *J. dent. Res.*, **31**, 319.

46. MULCAHY, R., and KNAGGS, J. F. (1968). 'Effect of age, parity and cigarette smoking on outcome of pregnancy.' *Am. J. Obstet. Gynec.*, **101**, 844.

47. PAFFENBARGER, R. S., WOLF, P. A., NOTKIN, J., and THORNE, M. C. (1966). 'Chronic disease in former college students. I. Early precursors of fatal coronary heart disease.' *Am. J. Epidem.*, **83**, 314.

48. PETERS, J. N., and FERRIS, B. G. (1967). 'Morphological constitution and smoking.' *Archs. envir. Hlth.*, **14**, 678.

49. PETERSON, F. J., and KELLEY, D. L. (1969). 'The effect of cigarette smoking upon the acquisition of physical fitness during training as measured by aerobic capacity.' *J. Am. Coll. Hlth. Assoc.*, **17**, 250.

50. PINDBORG, J. J. (1951). 'Gingivitis in military personnel with special reference to ulceromembranous gingivitis.' *Odont. Tidskr.*, **59**, 403.

51. REGISTRAR GENERAL (1968). *Statistical Review of England and Wales for the Year 1967.* Part. I. Tables, Medical. HMSO, London, Table 9.

52. RUSSELL, C. S., TAYLOR, R., and MADDISON, R. N. (1966). 'Some effects of smoking on pregnancy.' *J. Obstet. Gynaec. Br. Commonw.*, **73**, 742.

53. RUSSELL, C. S., TAYLOR, R., and LAW, C. E. (1968). 'Smoking in pregnancy, maternal blood pressure, pregnancy outcome, baby weight and growth and other related factors. A prospective study.' *Br. J. prev. soc. Med.*, **22**, 119.

53a. RUSSELL, C. S. (1969). 'Another hazard of smoking.' *New Scient.*, **41**, 64.

54. SELTZER, C. C. (1968). 'Morphological constitution and smoking. A further validation.' *Archs. envir. Hlth.*, **17**, 143.

55. SMITH, A. D. M., and DUCKETT, S. (1965). 'Cyanide, vitamin B_{12}, experimental demyelination and tobacco amblyopia.' *Br. J. exp. Path.*, **46**, 615.

56. SOLOMON, H. A., PRIORE, R. L., and BROSS, I. D. J. (1968). 'Cigarette smoking and periodontal disease.' *J. Am. dent. Ass.*, **77**, 1081.

57. SUMMERS, C. J., and OBERMAN, A. (1968). 'Association of oral disease with 12 selected variables. II. Edentulism.' *J. dent. Res.*, **47**, 594.

58. UNDERWOOD, P., HESTER, L. L., LAFFITTE, T., and GREGG, K. V. (1965). 'The relationship of smoking to the outcome of pregnancy.' *Am. J. Obstet. Gynec.*, **91**, 270.

59. US PUBLIC HEALTH SERVICE (1964). *Smoking and Health.* Report of the Advisory Committee to the Surgeon General of the Public Health Service. Public Health Service Publication No. 1103. *a*, pp. 196, 205, 212; *b*, p. 218; *c*, p. 339; *d*, p. 342; *e*, p. 344.

60. US PUBLIC HEALTH SERVICE (1967). *The Health Consequences of Smoking.* Public Health Service Publication No. 1696. *a*, pp. 145–152; *b*, p. 153; *c*, p. 183; *d*, p. 184; *e*, p. 188.

61. US PUBLIC HEALTH SERVICE (1968). *The Health Consequences of Smoking.* 1968 Supplement to the 1967 Public Health Service Review. Public Health Service Publication No. 1696. p. 104.

62. US PUBLIC HEALTH SERVICE (1969). *The Health Consequences of Smoking.* 1969 Supplement to the 1967 Public Health Service Review. Public Health Service Publication No. 1696-2. *a*, p. 58; *b*, p. 77; *c*, p. 85.

63. WYNDER, E. L., BROSS, I. J., and DAY, E. (1956). 'A study of environmental factors in cancer of the larynx.' *Cancer, N.Y.*, **9**, 86.

64. WYNDER, E. L., BROSS, I. J., and FELDMAN, R. M. (1957). 'A study of the etiological factors in cancer of the mouth.' *Cancer, N.Y.*, **10**, 1300.

65. YERUSMALMY, J. (1964). 'Mother's cigarette smoking and survival of infant.' *Am. J. Obstet. Gynaec.*, **88**, 505.

66. YOUNG, I. M., and PUGH, L. G. C. E. (1963). 'The carbon monoxide content of foetal and maternal blood.' *J. Obstet. Gynaec. Br. Commonw.*, **70**, 681.

67. ZABRISKIE, J. R. (1963). 'Effect of cigarette smoking during pregnancy. Study of 2,000 cases.' *Obstet. and Gynec.*, **21**, 405.

8 The Smoking Habit

8. 1   Throughout history men have tried various ways of reducing anxiety, relieving boredom, and promoting happiness and sociability. To these ends they have taken a great variety of drugs such as alcohol, opium, marijuana, betel nuts, cocaine, and nicotine; and more recently synthetic sedatives and stimulants. The use of drugs with psychological effects has varied widely between different communities and from age to age. Cheap gin drinking in the early eighteenth century was controlled by a prohibitive tax, a measure which Parliament was petitioned to adopt by the Royal College of Physicians in 1725 [2]. The cocaine habit, which began to spread rapidly after the First World War, is now uncommon for no obvious reason, though drug taking has been increasing recently in many industrialised countries.

8. 2   Although tobacco has been persistently and increasingly used since it was introduced into Europe from America the ways in which it has been used have changed partly under the dictates of fashion [18]. In England, tobacco was first smoked in pipes, although snuff became fashionable in the eighteenth century. Now, cigarettes are almost universal. Women seldom used tobacco in any form until the advent of cigarettes. In the USA tobacco chewing predominated until the early part of this century, when, apparently as a result of vigorous propaganda and revulsion against spitting, it declined and is now uncommon, especially among younger people [13].

8. 3   In the past, prejudice rather than any clear evidence of benefit or injury to health has led either to advocacy or to condemnation of the tobacco habit. Now that modern cigarettes are known to be so injurious, every means must be

adopted to discourage this modern fashion of smoking.
8. 4　To help people to stop smoking* it is necessary **to**
understand the complex reasons why they begin, and why,
though some stop, most continue. Recent research in this
field has been mostly concerned with conscious motivation
which can be discovered by questionnaires. Very little is
known about unconscious motives and satisfactions, or the
pharmacological or biochemical basis of addiction.

Starting to Smoke [1, 31]
8. 5　Most smokers make their first experiments in childhood
or during adolescence. Less than 20 per cent of men who
smoke regularly begin after the age of 20. Girls used to begin
smoking much later than boys but now they lag behind by
only a year or two; but of those who are now regular smokers
60 per cent started after they were 20. At first there is a
period of experimentation based on curiosity, conformity, or
bravado, or in order to appear grown-up. Social pressures
encourage this, for most children who smoke regularly have
friends who also smoke. The example and attitude of parents
towards smoking can have an important influence. There is
evidence of psychological needs that outweigh the usually
unpleasant effects of the first few smokes; boys who smoke
regularly tend to be less successful at work and games than
those who do not and may wish to compensate by smoking
as a symbol of toughness and precocity. Social pressure is
increased when boys and girls leave school, where smoking is
a minority habit, to find that smoking is the rule among their
workmates: there are many more smokers among adolescents
who leave than among their contemporaries who stay at
school [44].

Establishment of the Smoking Habit
8. 6　Tolerance soon develops and dependence often follows.
The smoker finds the habit satisfying and begins to feel a
sense of deprivation or craving when he is without a cigarette.

---

* In this chapter smoking will be taken to imply cigarette smoking unless
stated otherwise since nearly all the studies to be discussed have dealt with this
form of smoking.

If regular smoking is established this is usually within a few years of the first experiment. It is not long before most smokers become aware of some disadvantages, chiefly of expense and impairment of health. That people continue smoking in the face of these disincentives points to the strength of the dependence that so readily sets in.

Reasons for the Smoking Habit

8. 7   Using an eighteen-item questionnaire on reasons for smoking [22], American experts have categorised cigarette smokers according to reasons they give for smoking: stimulation; pleasure; alleviation of anxiety, tension or anger; relief of craving for a smoke; or because it is a fixed habit indulged automatically without satisfaction. Most smokers score highly on two or more factors, showing the complexity of smoking motivation.

8. 8   Another, not incompatible, analysis has been based on an extensive survey of the motives of British smokers [31]. They were classified according to the sorts of occasion on which they were likely or unlikely to smoke. There were two broad groups: those in whom the habit seemed to be chiefly motivated by 'inner needs' (smoking when irritated, happy, or hungry, when alone or when working) and those in whom a social factor predominated (smoking in company and in order to gain confidence). The social factor was commoner in adolescents than in adults. A useful distinction was made between 'dissonant' smokers who would like to or had tried to stop but had failed, and 'consonant' smokers who were happy about their smoking and had no wish to give it up. Each group comprised about half of all smokers. The 'dissonant' group smoked more for 'inner need' or craving while the 'consonant' group more often mentioned social factors. Most ex-smokers had been 'consonant' smokers before they stopped. Their attitude towards the habit had often been altered by changing to a job where it was not allowed, or by acquiring a new circle of non-smoking friends. It was concluded that the smokers who could most easily be persuaded to change their habit by health education would be found among the 'consonant' smokers, many of whom

were neither heavily dependent nor so aware of its harmful effects.

8. 9 These reports have been based on statements by smokers, in reply to questionnaires. Their answers may not always be valid for they may be affected by expectation, suggestibility, and readiness to accept generally held beliefs. Objective studies to confirm the validity of classifications of smokers by their stated needs are required.

8. 10 There is little evidence regarding unconscious forces which might lead to smoking. Freud held that men for whom the region of the lips had sexual importance from their childhood would in adult life have a powerful motive for smoking [11]. Psycho-analysts tend to regard the habit as a substitute gratification, originally based on deprivation of the maternal breast at weaning [7]. In one study an association was found between the ability to stop smoking and the age of weaning. Those who stopped easily had been weaned at an average age of 8 months while those who were unable to stop had been weaned at an average of 4·7 months [30]. However, in another large enquiry no association was found between the habit of smoking by the age of seventeen and early oral activities such as thumb sucking, breast feeding, or late weaning [36].

Differences between Smokers and Non-Smokers

8. 11 *Inheritance.* Since school children and adolescents who do or do not take up smoking differ in many characteristics, inheritance, personality, and social environment may play a part in determining the habit. Twin studies have suggested a genetic component in that identical twins are more concordant in their smoking habits than non-identical twins [9, 12, 34, 41, 45], a contrast which is not due to greater similarity of environment, for it is discernible when the identical twins have been brought up apart.

8. 12 *Personality.* To identify smoking types many studies have been made of personality differences between those who do and do not smoke [15, 20, 23, 28, 32, 38, 43]. Smokers tend to be impulsive, arousal-seeking, danger-loving, risk-takers who are belligerent towards authority. They drink

more tea, coffee, and alcohol, and are more prone to car accidents, divorce, and changing of jobs. Some of these characteristics collectively imply a degree of extraversion. Cigarette smokers have been found, on average, to be more extraverted than non-smokers [4, 5, 6, 42]. Although the differences are highly significant statistically they are small and there is a great overlap between smokers and non-smokers, so that personality characteristics do not reliably predict which individuals will become cigarette smokers [5]. Claims that smokers tend to be more anxious, emotional, tense, and neurotic have not been substantiated [4, 5, 42].

8. 13 *Social factors.* These are a dominating influence in starting smoking and second only to pharmacological factors in its maintenance. There is a fairly consistent pattern [1, 20, 31, 37]. Social class, academic achievement, example, and precept in the family, friends, type of school, church attendance, and drinking habits are all related to prevalence of smoking. Thus, fifteen year olds who have left school are more than twice as likely to be smokers as those who remain at school [44], but this association is partly due to lower social class, inferior schooling, and poor academic achievement, which predispose to early school leaving. There is no doubt of the striking effect of social factors in the increasing adoption of smoking by women since the First World War.

Pharmacological Dependence

8. 14 The smoking habit certainly conforms to the definition of drug dependence given by Paton [33]: 'Drug dependence arises when, as a result of giving a drug, forces—physiological, biochemical, social or environmental—are set up which predispose to continued drug use'. There is evidence that dependence on tobacco results from the action of nicotine [8], which has a powerful action on the nervous system (paras 3. 15 to 3. 19). The similarity of its effects to those of smoking suggests that many smokers crave tobacco for the nicotine present in the smoke. The remarkable spread of smoking throughout the world and the difficulty that most smokers find in abstaining suggests that the craving has a pharmacological basis. Further studies are needed, parti-

cularly in relation to withdrawal symptoms (para 8. 18).

Stopping Smoking

8. 15   About one in five of regular smokers stop, often only temporarily, especially at younger ages. But few of those who have given up after the age of 50 begin again [14]. With advancing age there is a steady increase in the proportion of smokers who have given it up until, at the age of 70, it is estimated that about one in three of those who had ever smoked regularly have ceased to do so [31, 44].

8. 16   Many reasons are given for stopping and for having tried to stop [18, 19, 31, 46]. The commonest are risks to health, many minor and immediate effects such as cough, repeated colds, and breathlessness, being more prominent than the more remote risks of lung cancer and other serious illnesses [10, 31]. Most smokers need to experience symptoms from smoking or to be convinced of its ultimate dangers to be persuaded to abandon the habit on grounds of health. Less than half of those who try to stop because of symptoms say that it was on their doctor's advice, but these are only one in three of all those who have ever tried to give it up. Expense is the next most frequent reason for stopping; indeed, among adolescents it comes first. The influence of other people, the desire to show self-control and, especially among doctors, parents and teachers, to set a good example are other motives. Only rarely are the untidiness, smell, and inconvenience mentioned [31].

8. 17   The reasons for success or failure in attempting to stop are not clear [18, 46]. Most of those who succeed are 'consonant' smokers who are not strongly dependent, but dependent smokers may also succeed if their motivation is strong enough and if they are supported by members of their families or friends who no longer smoke [31]. Intelligent appreciation of the disadvantages of smoking appears to be important. This is shown by the high proportion of doctors, university graduate staff and, increasingly, men in social classes I, II, and III who have stopped smoking [44] (para 1. 10). Acceptance of the facts about the harmful effects of cigarette smoking provides a powerful motive for giving it up. There

appears to be no risk of addiction to other drugs in those who stop smoking. Nearly all drug addicts are cigarette smokers.

Withdrawal Effects

8. 18   Heavy smokers often report distress in the weeks after stopping. Apart from intense craving, withdrawal effects include depression, anxiety, irritability, restlessness, sleep disturbance, difficulty in concentration, altered time perception, and various gastro-intestinal symptoms [8, 26]. Objective physical withdrawal effects have also been demonstrated, including sleep disturbance, sweating, gastro-intestinal changes, drop in blood pressure and pulse rate [8, 26], impaired performance at simulated driving [16] and changes in the electroencephalogram [47]. Some of these effects may, however, be partly psychological and may not appear when the motive for abstaining is strong enough. There is evidence that craving for cigarettes is related to nicotine deprivation, for this can be relieved by injections of nicotine that are pleasurable to smokers but not to non-smokers [25], and cigarette consumption has been reduced more with the help of intravenous injections of nicotine than with saline injections [29].

Persuading Smokers to Stop

8. 19   The finding that about half of all smokers do not wish to stop and reject what they have heard of its risks as having no bearing on themselves points to the need for more convincing public education [31]. Smokers must cease ignoring and misrepresenting the issue and must be convinced that the danger may involve each one of them and not just other smokers with 'weak lungs' or those who smoke more than they do. There is evidence that while failure to induce fear impairs success, excess of fear may also fail [17, 24]. Subjects with high self-esteem respond better to fear, while those with less self-esteem may respond better to a milder message [27]. Too little has been done to emphasise the financial benefit and improvement in health and amenity that non-smokers enjoy. A far greater volume of well-designed information is

needed, with the aid of television and radio, the press, advertisements in cinemas and on hoardings, and statements in cigarette packages. A communication which gives both sides of an argument is more likely to be effective than one which is biased [3]. For maximum effect a communication should be within the latitude of acceptance of the recipient [21, 40]. If it is too close to the recipient's attitude there is little inclination for change and if the distance is too great there may be a rebound effect from disbelief. The effects of improved design of information must be continually monitored by its effects on the attitudes of smokers and on consequent changes in their habits. The questionnaire referred to in para 8. 7, with its associated explanations, is claimed to help smokers wishing to discontinue by enabling them to analyse their reasons for smoking and thus to take appropriate steps to deal with them.

Help for the Dependent Smoker

8. 20   There will always be many 'dissonant' smokers who wish to stop but are too firmly habituated to be able to do so without special assistance. These are those who need the help of specialised smoking withdrawal clinics. The immediate success rate reported by these clinics in the past has often been considerable, but the proportion passing through them who are still not smoking after one year has seldom been better than one in three and is often less [39, 48]. Some clinics have reported greater success, amounting to as much as 60 per cent after one year. Even a 30 per cent success rate at such clinics is a considerable achievement, because they deal with those who have failed to stop unaided. Variation reported between the success of patients seeing different doctors at one smoking withdrawal clinic provides an opening for developing more effective methods [33a].

8. 21   Methods tried hitherto, apart from simple counselling, include various drugs (e.g. lobeline, and tranquillisers), none of which has been found to be more helpful than a placebo. There are reports of isolated success with hypnotism, but others who have used this method are less optimistic. Group

therapy, aversion therapy [35], and other forms of behaviour therapy have been employed, but the number of cases and the inadequacy of controls seldom permits any judgement of their value [39]. There is great need for further investigation into the most effective ways of helping dependent smokers.

Social Environment

8. 22   Over half of those who have ever given up say they began again because of the influence of family or friends who were still smoking [31]. The almost universal attitude that the habit is an innocuous and acceptable part of normal living must be altered if it is to be easier for smokers who stop to maintain their resolve. The desired change could be a natural consequence of increasing numbers of people who have succeeded in stopping and could be helped by greater restrictions in public transport and places of entertainment. It would also be helpful if, for instance, speakers on television programmes did not smoke during their appearances and if non-smoking households did not keep cigarettes to offer to their visitors. The more smokers who abandon the habit the greater will be their influence on those who continue. It is likely that once a noticeable trend from cigarette smoking has begun it will be self-propagating, for this appears to be happening in the USA [10a].

REFERENCES

1. BYNNER, J. M. (1969). *The Young Smoker*. A study of smoking among schoolboys, carried out for the Ministry of Health. SS 383. HMSO, London.
2. CHARLES, J. (1955). 'The contrivance of collegiation.' *Lancet*, 2, 987.
3. COHEN, A. R. (1964). *Attitude Change and Social Influence*. Basic Books, London.
4. EYSENCK, H. J. (1963). 'Smoking, personality, and psychosomatic disorders.' *J. psychosom. Res.*, 7, 107.
5. EYSENCK, H. J. (1965). *Smoking, Health and Personality*. Weidenfeld and Nicolson, London.
6. EYSENCK, H. J., TARRANT, M., WOOLF, M., and ENGLAND, L. (1960). 'Smoking and personality.' *Br. med. J.*, 1, 1456.
7. FENICHEL, O. (1954). *Collected Papers. First series*. Routledge and Kegan Paul, London. p. 233.
8. FINNEGAN, J. K., LARSON, P. S., and HAAG, H. B. (1945). 'The Role of nicotine in the cigarette habit.' *Science, N.Y.*, 102, 94.
9. FISHER, R. A. (1958). 'Cancer and smoking,' *Nature, Lond.*, 182, 596.

10. FLETCHER, C., and DOLL, R. (1969). 'A survey of doctors' attitudes to smoking.' *Br. J. prev. soc. Med.*, **23**, 145.

10a. FLETCHER, C. M., and HORN, D. (1970). 'Smoking and health.' *WHO Chronicle*, **24**, 345.

11. FREUD, S. (1949). *Three Essays on the Theory of Sexuality*. Trans. J. Strachey. Imago, London.

12. FRIBERG. L., KAIJ, L., DENCKER, S. J., and JONSSON, E. (1959). 'Smoking habits of monozygotic and dizygotic twins.' *Br. med. J.*, **1**, 1090.

13. HAMMOND, E. C., and GARFINKEL, L. (1961). 'Smoking habits of men and women.' *J. natn. Cancer Inst.*, **27**, 419.

14. HAMMOND, E. C., and GARFINKEL, L. (1964). 'Changes in cigarette smoking.' *J. natn. Cancer Inst.*, **33**, 49.

15. HEATH, C. W. (1958). 'Differences between smokers and non-smokers,' *Arch, intern. Med.*, **101**, 377.

16. HEIMSTRA, N. W., BANCROFT, N. R., and DEKOCK, A. R. (1967). 'Effects of smoking upon sustained performance in a simulated driving task.' *Ann. N.Y. Acad. Sci.*, **142**, 295.

17. HIGBEE, K. L. (1969). 'Fifteen years of fear arousal: Research on threat appeals: 1952–68.' *Psychol. Bull.*, **72**, 426.s

18. HORN, D. (1968). 'Some factors in smoking and its cessation.' In *Smoking, Health and Behaviour*. Ed. Borgatta, E. F., and Evans, R. R. Aldine Publishing Co., Chicago, p. 12.

19. HORN, D. (1969). 'Man, cigarettes and the abuse of gratification.' *Int. J. Addict.*, **4**, 471.

20. HORN, D., COURTS, F. A., TAYLOR, R. M., and SOLOMON, E. S. (1959). 'Cigarette smoking among high school students.' *Am. J. publ. Hlth.*, **49**, 1497.

21. HOVLAND, C. I., HARVEY, O. J., and SHERIF, M. (1957). 'Assimilation and contrast effects in reactions to communication and attitude change.', *J. abnorm. soc. Psychol.*, **55**, 244.

22. IKARD, F. F., GREEN, D. E., and HORN, D. (1969). 'A scale to differentiate between types of smoking as related to the management of affect.', *Int. J. Addict.*, **4**, 649.

23. JACOBS, M. A., ANDERSON, L. S., CHAMPAGNE, E., KARUSH, N., RICHMAN, S. J., and KNAPP, P. H. (1966). 'Orality, impulsivity and cigarette smoking in men.' *J. nerv. ment. Dis.*, **143**, 207.

24. JANIS, I. L., and TERWILLIGER, R. F. (1962). 'An experimental study of psychological resistances to fear arousing communications.' *J. abnorm. soc. Psychol.*, **65**, 403.

25. JOHNSTON, L. M. (1942). 'Tobacco smoking and nicotine.' *Lancet*, **2**, 742.

26. KNAPP, P. H., BLISS, C. M., and WELLS, H. (1963). 'Addictive aspects in heavy cigarette smoking.' *Am. J. Psychiat.*, **119**, 966.

27. LEVENTHAL, H. (1968). 'Experimental studies of anti-smoking communications.' In *Smoking, Health and Behaviour*. Ed. Borgatta, E. F., and Evans, R. R. Aldine Publishing Co., Chicago. p. 95.

28. LILIENFELD, A. M. (1959). 'Emotional and other characteristics of cigarette smokers and non-smokers as related to epidemiological studies of lung cancer and other diseases.' *J. natn. Cancer Inst.*, **22**, 259.

29. LUCCHESI, B. R., SCHUSTER, T. R., and EMLEY, G. S. (1967). 'The role of nicotine as a determinant of cigarette smoking frequency in man with observations of certain cardiovascular effects associated with the tobacco alkaloid.' *Clin. Pharmac. Ther.*, **8**, 789.

30. MCARTHUR, C., WALDRON, E., and DICKINSON, J. (1958). 'The psychology of smoking.' *J. abnorm. soc. Psychol.*, **56**, 267.

31. MCKENNELL, A. C., and THOMAS, R. K. (1967). *Adults' and Adolescents' Smoking Habits and Attitudes.* A report on a survey carried out for the Ministry of Health. 55353/B. HMSO. London.

32. MATARAZZO, J. D., and SASLOW, G. (1960). 'Psychological and related characteristics of smokers and non-smokers.' *Psychol. Bull.*, **57**, 493.

33. PATON, W. D. M. (1969). In *Scientific Basis of Drug Dependence.* Ed. Steinberg, J., J. & A. Churchill, London, p. 3.

33*a.* PINCHERLE, G., and WRIGHT, H. B. (1970). Smoking habits of business executives. Doctor variation in reducing cigarette consumption. *Practitioner*, **205**, 209.

34. RAASCHOU-NIELSEN (1960). 'Smoking habits in twins.' *Dan. med. Bull.*, **7**, 82.

35. RUSSELL, M. A. H. (1970). 'Effect of electric aversion on cigarette smoking.' *Br. med. J.*, **1**, 82.

36. SALBER, E. J. (1964). 'Infant orality and smoking.' *J. Am. med. Ass.*, **187**, 368.

37. SALBER, E. J., and ABELIN, T. (1967). 'Smoking behavior of Newton school children—5 year follow-up.' *Pediatrics*, **40**, 363.

38. SCHUBERT, D. S. P. (1959). 'Impulsivity and other personality characteristics of cigarette smokers.' *Am. J. Psychol.*, **14**, 354.

39. SCHWARTZ, J. L. (1969). 'A critical review and evaluation of smoking control methods.' *Publ. Hlth. Rep., Wash.*, **84**, 483.

40. SHERIF, M., and HOVLAND, C. I. (1961). *Social Judgement.* Yale University Press.

41. SHIELDS, J. (1966). *Monozygotic Twins.* Oxford University Press, London, p. 123.

42. SMITH, G. M. (1967). 'Personality correlates of cigarette smoking in students of college age.' *Ann. N.Y. Acad. Sci.*, **142**, 308.

43. STRAITS, B. C., and SECHREST, L. (1963). 'Further support of some findings about the characteristics of smokers and non-smokers.' *J. consult. Psychol.*, **27**, 282.

44. TODD, G. F. (1969). 'Statistics of smoking in the United Kingdom.' Tobacco Research Council Research Paper No. 1. Fifth edition, Table 54.

45. TODD, G. F., and MASON, J. I. (1959). 'Concordance of smoking habits in monozygotic and dizygotic twins.' *Heredity, Lond.*, **13**, 417.

46. TRAHAIR, R. C. S. (1967). 'Giving up cigarettes: 222 case studies.' *Med. J. Aust.*, **1**, 929.

47. ULETT, J. A., and ITIL, T. M. (1969). 'Quantitative electro-encephalogram in smoking and smoking deprivation.' *Science, N.Y.*, **164**, 969.

48. WAKEFIELD, J. (Ed.) (1969). *Influencing Smoking Behaviour.* A report of the Committee for Research in Smoking Habits appointed by the Norwegian Cancer Society. UICC Technical Report Series, Geneva. Vol. 3, p. 67.

9 *Prevention of Diseases Due to Smoking*

The Balance Between Benefit and Harm

9.1 The benefits which people say they derive from smoking are psychological and social. They claim that smoking provides solace in loneliness or distress, tranquillity when agitated or anxious, stimulation for action or work, and ease on social occasions. Of adult smokers in 1964, 90 per cent also agreed that the habit was pleasurable, but 60 per cent said that it cost more than the pleasure was worth [16b]. The world-wide growth of the habit in the past three centuries and the immense difficulty that many smokers find in giving up the habit are evidence of the hold it has on its devotees, which is probably due to the effects of nicotine.

9.2 The experience of many who have stopped shows that the benefits claimed are more easily dispensed with than expected, and many are pleased to be freed from their previous dependence.

9.3 The pleasures and benefits of smoking have to be weighed against its injurious consequences. The evidence presented in this Report shows that cigarette smokers have an increased risk of developing and of dying prematurely from diseases, chiefly lung cancer, bronchitis, emphysema and coronary heart disease, which are caused or aggravated by harmful substances in the cigarette smoke to which they are so frequently exposed. The increased risk of developing these smoking-related diseases is gradually lost over a period of ten or more years if cigarette smoking is stopped. Those who smoke only pipes or cigars in moderation have risk of illness that is only slightly greater than that of non-smokers.

The Need for Preventive Measures

9. 4   There can now be no doubt where the balance between benefit and harm from smoking lies. The habit is so costly to so many people in health and life, and to the country in financial loss (Appendix A), that remedial action is urgently needed. Only a change in smoking habits can prevent this national wastage. There are many who believe that a reduction in pollution of the air of our cities and towns would confer greater benefit on the public health than any interference with smoking habits. This has been discussed in another report from the Royal College of Physicians [19] from which it is clear that air pollution is a much less serious hazard to life and health than cigarette smoking. Perhaps the most striking evidence on this matter is provided by the fatal effects of cigarette smoking in country districts in Britain, in the Channel Islands [6], and in countries such as Scandinavia and Finland [18], where there is little air pollution. Action to protect the public against the damage done to so many of them by cigarette smoking would have more effect upon the public health in this country than anything else that could now be done in the whole field of preventive medicine.

9. 5   It is, of course, impracticable to prohibit a habit to which so many people are devoted, for this would lead to large scale evasion with consequences that could be as grave as were those of the prohibition of alcoholic drinks in the USA. While maintaining individual freedom of choice, every effort must be devoted to persuading smokers of cigarettes to take the only sure means of reducing the risks they run, which is to give up smoking. At the same time the tobacco manufacturers must be encouraged in their efforts to develop products that will not be so injurious as modern cigarettes, so that the dangers to those who cannot or do not wish to discontinue the habit may be diminished.

Identification of High-risk Smokers

9. 6   If it were possible to identify confidently those especially at risk, preventive measures could be confined to them. This cannot yet be done. A smoker's cough or evidence of abnormal lung function may be a warning of lung cancer, bronchi-

tis or emphysema (paras 4. 17 and 5. 16); cigarette smoking is particularly hazardous to those with such symptoms or with characteristics indicating an increased risk of coronary heart disease (para 6. 8). Pregnant women (para 7. 1) and people with gastric or duodenal ulcers (para 7. 11) are also especially vulnerable, but the ill effects of the habit are not limited to them. Effective prevention of diseases associated with smoking requires measures of general application.

Discouragement of Cigarette Smoking

9. 7 The connection between smoking and cancer of the lung and other diseases has been widely discussed in the press, on radio, and on television. Yet, ten years ago, a survey in Edinburgh showed that while almost everyone had heard of the connection only one in three believed that cigarette smoking could cause lung cancer [4]. In 1962, publication of the first report on smoking and health by the Royal College of Physicians was followed by much publicity about the hazards of smoking, but in 1964 a national survey confirmed that while almost everyone knew of the risks they underestimated their magnitude and relevance to themselves. Every year lung cancer kills over four times as many people as do road accidents, but three-quarters of all smokers thought that road deaths were more numerous [16*e*]. Over 80 per cent of smokers mistakenly thought that 'smog and fumes' were more important causes of lung cancer than cigarette smoking [16*d*].

9. 8 The percentage of adult smokers who believed or did not believe that smokers were likely to contract various conditions is shown in Table 9. 1 [16*c*]. The large majority agreed that smoking could cause cough and breathlessness, only one half that it could lead to lung cancer or bronchitis, and less than a quarter that it could be associated with heart disease or stomach ulcers. Most smokers who admitted any danger to health considered that it applied only to those who smoked more than they did. Table 9. 1 also shows the number of cigarettes per day above which most smokers who admitted any risk believed that it began; this was at such a high level of smoking as to represent a virtual denial of any

TABLE 9. 1

*Percentage opinions of adult smokers in 1964 on the risk of smokers suffering
from various conditions compared with the risk of non-smokers,
and the number of cigarettes per day at which the majority thought the risk started*

Opinion	Breath-lessness	Cough	Catarrh	Bron-chitis	Heart disease	Lung cancer	Stomach ulcer
Risk greater for smokers	79	85	46	51	22	50	19
Risk not greater for smokers	16	12	40	38	48	31	63
Don't know	5	3	14	11	30	19	18
Median no. of cigarettes/day for risk to appear*	15	15	15	15	20	25	15

* Opinion of those considering that smokers had a greater risk.

danger from heart disease or lung cancer. Most smokers even thought that bronchitis was likely to affect only exceptionally heavy cigarette smokers. This enquiry revealed two important errors which led many smokers to reject the evidence: 86 per cent of them believed that the experts differed among themselves about lung cancer [16e], and 30 per cent that doctors smoked as much as other people [16f].

9. 9   The need now is not merely to tell those who smoke that there is a *connection* between cigarette smoking and disease but to convince them that even so-called moderate cigarette smoking does cause disease, and that they themselves are in danger but can reduce the risk by changing their habits. They must be persuaded to face the issue of smoking and health. The evidence must be presented in a way which will produce more conviction of its truth and its relevance to individual health and happiness.

9. 10   It is necessary to challenge and change the present general acceptance of cigarette smoking as a harmless, fashionable, and even useful habit approved by government as an essential source of revenue. Public disapproval of a

dangerous habit that upsets many non-smokers must be promoted. Such a change of attitude has already been achieved in some circles. At conferences of consultant physicians it is now exceptional to find more than one or two individuals smoking a cigarette even during coffee breaks or at receptions. In the United States, where one in every three men and one in every four women who were smoking in 1966 had stopped by mid-1970 [8*b*], a climate of opinion is growing 'in which it becomes easier for others to stop' [8*a*].

9. 11   It is also necessary to develop better means of helping smokers who wish to stop but fail, and those who continue to smoke cigarettes must be encouraged to adopt less dangerous forms of smoking.

Public Education

9. 12   *The doctor's role.* Doctors have a unique opportunity for preventing common, dangerous, and disabling diseases by persuading their patients to give up cigarette smoking. Their special responsibility needs no emphasis. People go to their doctors for advice and are ready to listen. They often have respiratory disease or some other condition requiring abstinence from smoking. Once achieved temporarily, this could become established. But these opportunities for education and persuasion appear to have been much neglected. In 1964, of smokers who had ever tried to give up smoking for medical reasons, only 43 per cent said they had done so on their doctor's advice, and 80 per cent of smokers denied that any doctor had ever advised them to cut down or abandon the habit [16*a*].

9. 13   There are two aspects of the doctor's responsibilities. First, there is the example he sets. A doctor has a special responsibility because of the effect that his smoking habits have upon his patients and upon all those with whom he comes into contact. Many smokers base their denial of the risks on their observation of the minority of doctors who smoke.

9. 14   Second, medical men should take every appropriate opportunity to enquire into smoking habits of their patients and to tell all those who smoke, especially those (including

children) with early evidence of bronchitis (para 5. 16) or an increased risk of coronary heart disease (para 6. 8), about the risks of continuing and the benefits of stopping. This report may help doctors to advise patients effectively. The Department of Health in collaboration with the Health Education Council is producing pamphlets to help smokers to appreciate the risks they run, to analyse their reasons for smoking, and thus to indicate the best ways to stop.

9. 15. Many smokers will with this assistance discontinue with surprisingly little difficulty. Others who require more help may be referred to smoking-control clinics when these have been re-established (para 9. 36). Those who continue to smoke cigarettes should be advised to follow 'the rules for less dangerous smoking' (para 9. 47).

9. 16 Doctors working in organisations in which pre-employment or regular medical examinations are carried out have special opportunities for giving firm advice and help to anyone with a heightened risk of chest or heart disease.

Medical Education

9. 17 In 1965 the Social Survey found that just over one-half of male and one-third of female medical students in England and Wales were smokers, chiefly of cigarettes [2]. The proportion was less than among the general public but the same as among non-medical students. There was a small but temporary decrease in smoking during the first clinical year. Sixty-seven per cent of pre-clinical and 44 per cent of clinical students denied that their teachers had made any attempt to dissuade them from smoking, and half of them said they were allowed to smoke in lectures. Less than half of the smoking students believed that doctors should set an example to their patients or to the public in respect of smoking, and a quarter considered that they should not even advise their own patients not to smoke. They were quite well-informed about the diseases to which smokers are liable but ill-informed about the degree of the risk and the nature of the evidence. Forty-two per cent thought that more people died from road accidents each year than from lung cancer. Only 50 per cent of clinical students who smoked (compared with

70 per cent of those who did not) agreed that smoking was a cause of lung cancer. The chief reason for rejecting the evidence was that it was 'only statistical' (para 4. 24).

9. 18   It is clear from this report that although medical students are being taught about the risks of cigarette smoking they are not all being convinced by their teachers of their responsibilities for reducing these risks: they are not being urged to avoid smoking or being trained to play any part in the education of their patients in this matter. The teaching staff of medical schools must correct this state of affairs.

Publicity on Smoking and Health

9. 19   Anti-smoking posters, such as those representing smokers as sheep, or as prisoners, have been based on ideas about smoking that are far removed from those of most people. One poster depicted an ashtray full of dirty cigarette stubs against a newspaper headline about increasing lung cancer deaths. Many smokers took this to imply that those at risk were only those who smoked more heavily than themselves and who were messy people. Posters, in any case, can provide no more than a background for altering public attitudes.

9. 20   Although the dangers of cigarette smoking have often been mentioned on television and radio, there has been no planned series of broadcasts intended to persuade and help people to give it up. Three short films have been produced for television but have seldom been shown at peak viewing hours. In the USA, television advertisements of cigarettes have continued to appear* but in September 1967 the Federal Communications Commission upheld its ruling under a 'fairness doctrine' that any radio or television station accepting cigarette advertising had to devote a related amount of time to the hazards of cigarette smoking [8a]. The consequent frequent broadcasting of such warnings appears to have had a big impact on smoking habits. The Canadian Parliamentary Committee on Tobacco and Cigarette Smoking has recommended that there should be 'increased use of smoking and

* Advertisements of cigarettes on television will be prohibited after the end of 1970 in the U.S.A.

health commercials on television and radio as compulsory prime-time public service announcements' [15]. The Government should consult the broadcasting authorities and newspaper proprietors about ways in which more regular and effective publicity could be given to the facts about smoking and health, to the importance of abstaining from cigarette smoking, and to ways in which smokers can best manage to do this.

9. 21   A more personal and direct approach than that of posters and broadcasts could be useful. The doctors' contribution has already been emphasised. In 1965, the British Medical Association delivered a pamphlet on simple questions of health to every household in the country and it had a considerable impact. There is much to be said for general distribution of a statement of the advantages of being a non-smoker and about ways by which smokers might stop.

Education of Children

9. 22   Since it is easier not to start smoking than to stop, stress has been laid on teaching children about the dangers of smoking. This should be aimed at increasing the respect of children for the non-smokers among them. Its effectiveness will increase as more adults give up smoking and set an example to children, strongly influenced as they are by their parents, their older brothers and sisters, and their teachers. But children can also influence their parents, some of whom have reported that they have discontinued smoking because of their children's concern for their health.

9. 23   In 1964, 66 per cent of boys at secondary modern schools but only 47 per cent at grammar schools and 44 per cent at comprehensive schools said they had had some form of health education on smoking. There was no evidence that smoking was less common in schools where health education had been given than in the others, or that any particular method was more successful than any other [3]. It might be thought that the ultimate dangers of smoking would appear too remote to influence children, but in one American investigation it was found that information about these risks was more effective than emphasis on the immediate dis-

advantages [13a]. In a British study, however, the reverse was found [12]. Suggestions for improving the present ineffective methods were developed from the survey of schoolboys' attitudes to smoking [3] and these should be tried.

9. 24   Training colleges provide teachers with little information about the harmful effects of smoking cigarettes or about methods whereby they could discourage their pupils from smoking. Children are unlikely to take much notice of teachers who tell them about the harm done by cigarettes but disregard it themselves.

9. 25   The Department of Education and Science is now collaborating with the Department of Health and Social Security and the Health Education Council to develop more effective ways of training teachers and educating children on matters of health in general including the effects of cigarette smoking. This collaborative study should be given every encouragement in order that smoking by schoolchildren may be cut down.

9. 26   Most children obtain their cigarettes from shops but one in five of the younger children who smoke get them from vending machines. Further consideration should be given to strengthening and extending the regulations that forbid selling cigarettes to children and to the abolition of all cigarette-vending machines in public places. This would not only make it less easy for children to acquire cigarettes but also show that the community is determined to discourage young people from starting a really dangerous habit.

Cigarette Advertising

9. 27   The British tobacco manufacturers claim that their advertisements and coupon schemes neither encourage people to begin smoking nor smokers to smoke more, but only promote particular brands among existing smokers. They have voluntarily agreed to avoid types of advertisement that appeared to induce young people to take to cigarettes (para 1. 12). Banning cigarette advertisements from television was not followed by any general reduction in smoking but it was accompanied by a great increase of gift coupon schemes that could have nullified any effect of the ban.

Increased expenditure on sales promotion has not been associated with any great increase in cigarette consumption.

9. 28   That a simple ban of cigarette advertising would be ineffective is also indicated by the example of countries such as Russia [9] and Italy [1] where there is no advertising of cigarettes and where consumption has steadily risen. Nevertheless, it is unwise to allow any form of promotion of a habit with such grave effects on health. The mere existence of advertisements for cigarettes implies that they are desirable and harmless. This contributes to the cultural acceptability of the smoking habit and conflicts with the credibility of public education about its dangers. Those attending anti-smoking clinics have complained that cigarette advertisements tend to weaken their resolve.

9. 29   The Committee of the Norwegian Cancer Society has recommended the 'preparation of legislation to reduce the volume of tobacco advertising as far in the direction of a total ban on advertising as will be practically enforceable' [21]. The Canadian Standing Committee on Tobacco and Cigarette Smoking has advocated legislation to enforce a gradual reduction of advertising ending with 'complete elimination of all cigarette promotional activities' within a four year period [15]. Both these recommendations were reached after lengthy consideration of the effects of cigarette advertising.

9. 30   All forms of cigarette advertising (excluding only displays at point-of-sale) and of gift-coupon schemes with cigarettes should be prohibited. This would provide a clear declaration of Parliament's concern about the dangers of the habit and about the need for unimpeded public education about it.

Smoking in Public Places

9. 31   A useful contribution to changing public attitudes might be made if it were less easy for people to smoke when travelling and in places of entertainment. The Government's reluctance to impose such restrictions despite evidence that a large proportion of the public would find them acceptable has already been referred to (para 1. 16). What is required

is a change of attitude by the Government and Transport Authorities rather than by the public. Cigarette smoking is almost encouraged in aeroplanes and provision for non-smokers is seldom made. Since at least one half of air passengers are now non-smokers there is a strong case for protecting them against the inconvenience of their neighbours' smoking. It is difficult to believe that this would really be impracticable.

9. 32   Some large retail stores have banned smoking on their premises. More might be done here and in other places of work. In view of the fire risk of smoking and the greater sickness absence rates of smokers compared with non-smokers, employers might improve their own productivity, the safety of their premises, and their employees' health by banning smoking at work. Food and chemical manufacturing firms already do this. Employers' organisations and Trade Unions should examine this question and make proposals for wider restrictions on smoking at work. Universities should consider a general prohibition of smoking in lectures and laboratories.

Reduced Life Insurance Premiums for Non-smokers

9. 33   It appears unfair that non-smokers, with their greater life expectancy than cigarette smokers, should be charged the same premiums for life insurance. In this country some insurance companies when approached about this appear to be unaware of the large differences in the risks of smokers and non-smokers; others reply that it is against their policy to offer differential premiums. They also doubt the accuracy of the replies they would obtain about smoking habits although they act upon the answers to other questions that are probably more liable to error. A few American insurance companies are now offering reduced premiums to non-smokers, an example which British companies should be urged to follow.

Warnings on Cigarette Packages and on Advertisements

9. 34   Since January 1966 all cigarette packages in USA have been required to carry a warning notice: 'Caution: cigarette smoking may be hazardous to your health'. Such

an indefinite warning could not be expected to influence the smoker and was not violently opposed by the American tobacco industry. Surveys of public opinion in the USA have shown that only one in five people said that he or she had been affected by it, and only 2 per cent had consequently stopped or decided not to start smoking [13]. A more definite notice is now to be introduced [8a]: 'Warning: the Surgeon-General has determined that cigarette smoking is dangerous to your health'. A first reading in the House of Commons has been given to a Private Member's Bill to provide for the labelling of cigarette packets: 'Danger. These cigarettes can harm your health. Cigarettes are known to cause lung cancer, bronchitis and heart disease' [10].

9. 35　A bill of this kind should be passed and consequent effects on smokers' attitudes and habits assessed. The impact of such a warning might be strengthened by enclosing within each packet a card giving brief advice for persistent smokers on ways in which they could reduce the risks they run (para 9. 43). If advertisements are allowed to continue, legislation to insist on them including warnings on the danger of smoking should be considered.

Help for the Unwilling Smoker

9. 36　Since approximately one half of those who smoke cigarettes in Britain say that they would like to give them up but have failed to do so and since one in five of doctors continue to smoke cigarettes despite their knowledge of the dangers (para 1. 10), it is evident that education and experience alone are not enough. Special help is needed for some of those who want to stop, or who must do so for medical reasons. Many smokers who wish to abandon the habit fail to do so because they are not really convinced of the necessity, and they have therefore never taken the decision. Others have never analysed their reasons for smoking or considered alternative sources for the satisfaction they derive from the habit. Such smokers may be helped by the pamphlets referred to in para 9. 14. There will, however, remain a large number of unwilling smokers who need the help of special smoking control clinics.

9. 37   The small number of clinics set up by enthusiastic doctors to help unwilling smokers after publication of the first Report of the Royal College of Physicians on Smoking and Health in 1962, received little official help or encouragement and almost all have been discontinued. A change of policy is required. The Department of Health and Social Security should set up a joint committee with the Medical Research Council to advise on staff, techniques, record keeping, and research in such clinics. If this were done, techniques might become more effective, and smoking control clinics could be established not only in hospitals and health departments but also in factories and offices.

Less Dangerous Forms of Smoking

9. 38   *Pipes and cigars.* The remarkable disparity of risk between smokers of cigarettes and smokers of pipes and cigars (para 2. 2) suggests that much saving of life and health might be achieved if cigarette smokers were to change to pipes or cigars. Unfortunately, no study has yet been made on the health of those who have made this change. Cigarette smokers, accustomed to inhaling, might continue to inhale the smoke of pipe and cigars and to smoke heavily enough to maintain the risk. That the change is likely to be beneficial is suggested by the experience of many individual cigarette smokers who report that on changing to pipes or cigars their cough diminishes. But judgement must be reserved since there are reports from Europe suggesting an incidence of lung cancer as great in pipe and cigar smokers as in cigarette smokers (para 4. 13), and since in parts of Europe where most of the cigarettes are made of sun-cured tobacco (thought to be less dangerous) mortality from lung cancer among smokers is high [7]. The likelihood of benefit is, however, great enough for this change to be encouraged in those who cannot stop.

9. 39   *Cigarettes with reduced nicotine and 'tar' content.* Absorption of nicotine from cigarettes may be responsible for the increase of cardiovascular disease in cigarette smokers (para 3. 20) and it may be the basis for many smokers' dependence on the habit (para 3. 19). Since the only cancer-producing sub-

stances hitherto identified in tobacco smoke are contained in
the 'tar' fraction, cutting down the tar delivery of cigarettes
might lessen the danger of cancer; and since there is already
evidence from both human experience (para 4. 10) and from
animal experiments (paras 3. 4) that diminution of the
risk might result from the use of filtered cigarettes, there are
good grounds for reducing the tar and nicotine content of
cigarettes.

9. 40   The delivery of nicotine and tar in the smoke of a
single cigarette can be varied within wide limits by filters and
different varieties of tobacco leaf, and there is a great variation of tar and nicotine content of different brands. An analysis of 122 brands of cigarettes published by the US Federal
Trade Commission in October 1968 showed nicotine deliveries ranging from 0·12 to 2·3 mg per cigarette, a twenty-
fold range, and tar deliveries ranging from 4 to 36 mg, a
nine-fold range. Present British brands have a wide range from
0·4 to 3·0 mg of nicotine and from 8 to 31 mg of tar per cigarette (measured as particulate matter; water and nicotine free).
With very few exceptions plain cigarettes have higher tar and
nicotine deliveries than tipped cigarettes of comparable size.
The highest deliveries are from plain, King Size cigarettes,
but sales of these are now very small in Britain.

9. 41   The tar and nicotine content of the smoke of all
brands of cigarettes should be published and packets should
be labelled with this information. This would be justified, in
conformity with the Trades Description Act, on the simple
grounds that the customer should know the nature of the
article he buys. It would be necessary for official analyses to
be carried out periodically to check that the published
figures were correct within acceptable limits of variation.*

9. 42   If such information were to be provided, an authoritative medical statement would be needed on the significance
of the analyses in relation to health risks, indicating that
while the only sure way of avoiding them is not to smoke. The
risk might be less if cigarettes with low tar and nicotine con-

* The Consumer's Association states that it proposes to publish in the near
future details of the tar and nicotine content of major brands of cigarettes
available in the United Kingdom.

tent were smoked, so long as there was no increase in the tumour-producing activity of the tar nor in cigarette consumption. Surveys in America have demonstrated little tendency for smokers who change to lower nicotine and tar cigarettes to smoke more of them, to smoke more of each cigarette, or to inhale more [20]. An unpublished study by one British tobacco manufacturer suggests that only a minority (some 10 to 15 per cent) of smokers given cigarettes with a 50 per cent reduction of nicotine alter their ways of smoking so as to obtain more smoke from each.

9. 43   The reason for publishing this information would be to dissuade smokers from using those brands likely to be specially dangerous because of their high content of tar and nicotine. This purpose could be reinforced by imposing a a statutory upper limit on tar and nicotine content. The Canadian Committee on Tobacco and Cigarette Smoking has recommended that 'production of cigarettes exceeding specified maximum of tar and nicotine content' should be discontinued and that the levels set should be determined by what would be 'acceptable to most smokers' and should be 'progressively reduced as tolerated by society and techniologically feasible' [15].

9. 44   Too little is known at present about the medical significance of the many individual chemical components of the 'tar' and of the numerous compounds in the gaseous fraction of cigarette smoke to warrant publication of detailed analyses or advocating the use of special filters designed to eliminate particular gaseous fractions.

9. 45   The tar and nicotine content of all marketed brands of cigarettes should be published, displayed where they are sold, and printed on the packets, and a statement on the relation of these figures to the hazards of smoking should be made available to the public. The Government should start discussions with the tobacco manufacturers and medical authorities with a view to introducing a statutory upper limit of tar and nicotine delivery of cigarettes.

9. 46   All this could be done immediately, but the production of less dangerous cigarettes is a complicated matter. There have, for instance, been recent announcements of

tobacco substitutes which, incorporated into cigarettes, might reduce their harmful effect. Cigarettes which have been shown on biological tests to have reduced cancer-producing and irritant effects would have a different flavour from current brands and could be more expensive. Smokers would be unlikely to take to them without a strong incentive on the grounds of health or expense, and this incentive could not be given without a strong presumption of benefit. The Medical Research Council should assess the results of biological tests carried out by the tobacco industry on new smoking materials and conduct or sponsor research to determine the effects on health of those smoking modified cigarettes. The questions of what statements should be made about the effects of these and whether and by what means smokers should be encouraged to adopt them should be determined by a committee set up for this purpose with representatives of the Medical Research Council and the various Government Departments concerned (para 9. 53).

Less Dangerous Smoking Habits

9. 47   Those who are unable or do not want to stop smoking may reduce the risk by:

> smoking fewer cigarettes,
> inhaling less,
> smoking less of each cigarette,
> leaving a longer stub (for the concentration of tar and nicotine in the smoke increases as smoking proceeds),
> taking fewer puffs from each cigarette,
> taking the cigarette out of the mouth between puffs,
> smoking brands with a low content of tar and nicotine.

Encouragement of such habits among continuing smokers is important. Anyone who thus deliberately changes his habits has accepted the risks as relevant to himself and this is the first step towards the decision to stop. Inclusion of cards listing these 'less dangerous ways of smoking' in every cigarette packet might be an effective form of public health education. The Government should consider enacting legislation to ensure that this advice is given with every cigarette packet sold.

Tobacco Taxation

9. 48 Since expense is the commonest reason given by smokers for wishing to give up smoking an increase in the price of cigarettes would be expected to reduce smoking. The effects of small increases in the price of cigarettes have hitherto been only transient, and not much more is to be expected from further small rises. A large increase might be effective but would be undesirable in other respects. It would bear hardly on the many smokers with small incomes who are so habituated that they would continue to smoke as much as before and so spend less on essential family needs. It might also result in an increase in crime. Lorry loads of cigarettes already provide a tempting bait for criminals and the more expensive the cigarettes the more tempting they would be.

9. 49 A differential tax, increasing the retail price of cigarettes while reducing the price of pipe and cigar tobaccos, might induce many either to stop smoking, or if they could not do so to change to pipes or cigars. There should be little administrative difficulty in arranging a differential tax. All that is required is to reduce the tax of all tobacco out of bond and to impose a purchase tax on cigarettes. When the nicotine and tar content of cigarettes is published and when cigarettes that are considered on these and other grounds to be likely to be less dangerous are marketed (para 9. 46), a differential tax to reduce their cost should be considered. A price differential in favour of low nicotine cigarettes has already increased their use in Austria [17]. If nicotine is the basis for tobacco habituation a trend to smoking cheaper cigarettes with a lower nicotine content might reduce the degree of dependence in established smokers and make it less likely that children starting to smoke would become habituated.

9. 50 Such tax differentials would reduce the total yield of tobacco revenue if many smokers changed to lower taxed forms of smoking or were persuaded by this evidence of parliamentary concern about the dangers of cigarette smoking to give it up altogether. Ministers from both the main political parties have indicated their unwillingness to reduce this source of revenue (para 1. 20). Indeed the Treasury has

already met the possibility of the incorporation in cigarettes of substances other than tobacco by legislation in the Finance Act of 1970 to ensure that such substances should be taxed at the same rate as tobacco without, so far as is known, any consideration of the health aspects of the matter. Apart from the large financial cost to the community of cigarette smoking (Appendix A) the issue is in essence quite simple. Government and Parliament have to decide between an easy source of revenue and the preservation of the lives, health, and productive capacity of the people they serve. To ensure proper consideration of this aspect the Treasury should have the continued advice of specially appointed advisory committees (para 9. 53).

9. 51   An official enquiry should be carried out into the economic consequences of a decrease in cigarette smoking and a full, public account of the balance of benefit and loss should be published. Official estimates of this balance in the USA and Canada, both of which countries have large investments in tobacco production and manufacture, show that elimination of cigarette smoking would result in greater savings than losses [5, 11]. It is very likely that in this country there would be a large credit balance (Appendix A).

Requirements for Success in the Prevention of Diseases due to Smoking

9. 52   If success in the control of smoking is really to be achieved the attack must be made on many fronts with a continual flow of information and encouragement to children and to adults. Education in schools and generally by the mass media and by booklets and pamphlets may heighten awareness of the risks of smoking but is unlikely to carry conviction without demonstration of Governmental concern by restrictions on advertising, warnings on cigarette packets, tax differentials, and restriction of smoking in public places. Example and personal advice by doctors are needed to affect the individual decision to give up the habit. Once adult smoking has begun to decline the social environment will change to one in which smokers will wish to stop and will find it easier to do so, and in which fewer children will wish to become smokers.

9. 53 This campaign for the prevention of preventable diseases will require effective organisation. The Royal College of Physicians has taken the initiative in setting up a council of voluntary organisations to play their part. A standing Government Committee is also required to co-ordinate the activities of the various departments that are concerned. These include the Departments of Health and Social Security and of Education and Science, The Treasury, The Board of Trade, Customs and Excise, the Medical and Social Research Councils, and the Health Education Council. The aim of these co-ordinating bodies must be to ensure that within five years there is a measurable decline of deaths and disablement from diseases related to smoking, and that within a generation the harmful effects of smoking are no longer a matter for public concern.

9. 54 The Government and people of this country must decide to tackle the problems of smoking and health with determination. If this decision is taken, thousands of smokers, who would otherwise continue year after year to become ill and to die before their time, will enjoy longer and healthier lives.

Summary of Recommendations

1. Doctors should set an example by still greater abstinence from smoking and must take every opportunity to urge their patients not to smoke cigarettes. Instruction of medical students about the effects of smoking and their responsibilities in this matter must be improved (paras 9. 12 to 9. 18).

2. More effective public information about the health consequences of smoking must be achieved by every means and the Government should consult the Broadcasting Authorities and newspaper proprietors to achieve more effective publicity (paras 9. 19 to 9. 21).

3. Better means of educating children must be developed. Teachers should set an example to their pupils. Regulations forbidding the sale of cigarettes to children should be strengthened, and cigarette vending machines should be removed from public places (paras 9. 22 to 9. 26).

4. Advertisements of cigarettes and gift-coupon schemes should be prohibited (paras 9. 27 to 9. 30).
5. More restrictions on smoking in public transport and places of entertainment should be enforced (para 9. 31).
6. Employers' organisations and Trades Unions should agree on wider restrictions of smoking at work; universities should restrict smoking in lectures (para 9. 32).
7. Life insurance companies should consider reduced premiums for non-smokers (para 9. 33).
8. Warning notices should be printed on packets of cigarettes and, if they are allowed to continue, on cigarette advertisements (paras 9. 34, 9. 35).
9. More effective techniques for helping unwilling smokers to stop must be developed in special research clinics, and when this has been done smoking control clinics should be established in hospitals, health departments, factories, and offices (paras 9. 36, 9. 37).
10. The tar and nicotine content of all marketed brands of cigarettes should be published and a public statement made on the possible effects on health of smoking them. The Government should consider imposing statutory upper limits on the nicotine and tar content of cigarettes. The Medical Research Council should collaborate with the tobacco industry with regard to tests of cigarettes which are likely to be less hazardous and should conduct research to determine the effects on health of smoking such cigarettes (paras 9. 38 to 9. 46).
11. Those who continue to smoke should be encouraged, possibly by cards enclosed in cigarette packets:
   to smoke fewer cigarettes,
   to inhale less,
   to smoke less of each cigarette,
   to take fewer puffs from each cigarette,
   to take the cigarette out of the mouth between puffs,
   to smoke brands with low nicotine and tar content (para 9. 47).
12. The Government must look beyond an easy source of revenue to the reality of the injurious effects of modern cigarettes on the health and economy of the country; dif-

ferential taxation of tobacco products should be imposed to discourage more hazardous forms of smoking (paras 9. 48 to 9. 50).

13. An official enquiry should be made into the economic consequences of present smoking habits and of the results of a general reduction in cigarette smoking (para 9. 51).

14. A standing Government Committee to co-ordinate smoking control measures should be established.

15. Prevention of diseases caused by smoking can be achieved only if the attack is effectively organised on many fronts. These recommendations have as their goal the preservation of the lives and health of thousands of smokers who would otherwise continue year after year to become ill and to die before their time (paras 9. 52 to 9. 54).

REFERENCES

1. Beese, D. H. (Ed.) (1968). *Tobacco Consumption in Various Countries.* Tobacco Research Council Research Paper No. 6, 2nd edit. London.

2. Bynner, J. M. (1967). *Medical Students Attitudes Towards Smoking.* A report on a survey carried out for the Ministry of Health, SS 382. HMSO, London.

3. Bynner, J. M. (1969). *The Young Smoker.* A study of smoking among schoolboys, carried out for the Ministry of Health. SS 383. HMSO, London.

4. Cartwright, A., Martin, F. M., and Thomson, J. G. (1960). 'Health hazards of cigarette smoking; current popular beliefs.' *Brit. J. prev. soc. Med.,* 14, 160.

5. Canadian Department of National Health and Welfare (1967). 'The estimated cost of certain identifiable consequences of cigarette smoking upon health longevity, and property in Canada in 1966.' Research and Statistics Memo, Ottawa.

6. Dean, G. (1964). 'Lung cancer in South Africans and British immigrants.' *Proc. R. Soc. Med.,* 57, 984.

7. Doll, R. (1969). 'The geographical distribution of cancer.' *Brit. J. Cancer,* 23, 1.

8. Fletcher, C. M., and Horn, D. (1970). *a,* 'Smoking and Health'. *WHO Chronicle,* 24, 345. *b,* Horn, D. Personal communication.

9. Food and Agriculture Organisation of the United Nations (1969). Committee on commodity problems. Forty-fourth session. *Review of Trends and Problems in the World Tobacco Economy.* FAO, Rome.

10. Hansard (1970). Vol. 794, No. 42, Wednesday, 21st January, col. 519.

11. Hedrick, J. L. (1970). 'Economic costs of cigarette smoking.' The Resource Management Corporation of Bethesda, Md., USA (unpublished).

12. HOLLAND, W. W., and ELLIOTT, A. (1968). 'Cigarette smoking, respiratory symptoms and anti-smoking propaganda. An experiment.' *Lancet*, **1**, 41.

13. HORN, D. (1960). *a*, 'Modifying smoking habits in high school students.' *Children*, **7**, 63. *b*, personal communication.

14. IMPERIAL TOBACCO GROUP LIMITED (1969). *Cigarette Coupon Schemes and Cigarette Advertising.* Second edit.

15. ISABELLE, M. G. (1969). CANADA. STANDING COMMITTEE ON HEALTH WELFARE AND SOCIAL AFFAIRS ON TOBACCO AND CIGARETTE SMOKING. *First Report.* Queen's Printer, Ottawa.

16. MCKENNELL, A. C., and THOMAS, R. K. (1967). *Adults' and Adolescents' Smoking Habits and Attitudes.* A report on a survey carried out for the Ministry of Health. SS 353/B. HMSO, London. *a*, pp. 228 and 273; *b*, p. 257; *c*, pp. 265–269; *d*, p. 270; *e*, p. 271; *f*, p. 272; *g*, p. 221.

17. NATIONAL CLEARING HOUSE FOR SMOKING AND HEALTH (1969). *Smoking and Health Programmes in Other Countries.* US Dept. of Health Education and Welfare, Washington.

18. PEDERSEN, E., MAGNUS, K., MORK, T., HOUGEN, A., and BJELKE, E. (1969). 'Lung cancer in Finland and Norway.' *Acta. path. microbiol. scand.*, **76**, Suppl. 199.

19. ROYAL COLLEGE OF PHYSICIANS (1970). *Air Pollution and Health.* Pitman Medical, London.

20. WAINGROW, S., and HORN, D. (1968). 'Relationship of number of cigarettes smoked to "tar" rating.' *Natn. Cancer Inst. Monogr.* **28**, 29.

21. WAKEFIELD, J. (Ed.) (1969). *Influencing Smoking Behaviour.* A report of the Committee for Research in Smoking Habits appointed by the Norwegian Cancer Society. UICC Technical Report Series, Geneva. Volume 3.

Appendix A

Economic Consequences of a Reduction in Cigarette Smoking

A. 1 The facts that large numbers of premature deaths and wide-spread illness are caused by cigarette smoking and that their prevention demands vigorous action to persuade people not to smoke have important economic implications. Although it is not known whether any official assessment of these implications has been carried out, it appears that the government's failure to take any effective preventive action is based on the fear that the country can neither afford to lose the revenue derived from tobacco taxation nor tolerate the economic consequences of running down the tobacco industry. Unofficial assessments, however, suggest that this fear may be mistaken.

A. 2 In a review of the economic effects of tobacco sales [1], it was concluded that loss of employment from a gradual reduction of cigarette smoking sales would not present serious problems, for less than one worker out of every 200 in manufacturing industry was directly employed in manufacturing tobacco, and that even in the areas where this was heavily concentrated its disappearance would not create any major problems provided that this did not, as it would not, happen overnight. On the distribution side, about one worker in twenty in the retail trade would be displaced if tobacco sales were stopped, but many, being elderly and self-employed, would not seek new jobs. The main impact would be the disappearance of many thousands of small shops and probably a more expensive structure for distribution of newspapers and confectionery. If cigarette advertising were prohibited there would be 'some agonising reappraisals on both sides of the advertising account' but it was unlikely that elimination of tobacco advertisements would have the effect of compelling an increase in the price of newspapers and periodicals in general.

A. 3 The revenue from taxation of tobacco is thought to be an essential contribution to the national budget, but since smokers who stop smoking almost invariably spend on other goods the money saved it should not be difficult to derive revenue from this expenditure by appropriate forms of taxes on other goods. With regard to the balance of trade, it has been estimated that there would be a saving of £70 million on the country's visible trade account. Problems would be created in some countries from curtailment of tobacco imports but even so: 'the British contribution to the world economy arising from the country's smoking habits is not so great as to have more than local and secondary effects'.

A. 4 There is a great financial loss to the country and to many individuals from illness caused by cigarette smoking. There are the costs of hospital and other treatments, and incapacity to work with loss of production and loss of earnings, partly compensated by sickness benefits. To this must be added lifetime loss of production and earnings from premature deaths due to cigarette smoking and the consequent widows pensions. A recent estimate [2] of these losses due to lung cancer, bronchitis, and coronary heart disease attributable to cigarette smoking was £270 million per annum. On the credit side of the economic balance, reduction of cigarette smoking would prevent many fires. In 1964 it was estimated that some £10 million could be saved by prevention of fires due to smoking. Savings from reduction of these real costs to the country due to decrease of cigarette smoking would offset the inconvenience of seeking other sources of revenue than tobacco [1].

A. 5 Whatever steps might be taken to reduce cigarette smoking this reduction, and any economic consequences, would be gradual, and adjustments could be made when and as necessary. It must be born in mind that other tobacco products than modern cigarettes might be developed which would be free from their dangers but equally popular. If this happened, diseases due to cigarette smoking might be prevented without any economic disturbance, but it would be many years before the safety of any alternative forms of smoking could be established. Meanwhile it is clear that if smoking of present day cigarettes were greatly reduced the ultimate economic and social benefits would be much greater than the temporary economic inconvenience.

A. 6 It is desirable that an official enquiry should be carried out into the economic consequences of a decrease in cigarette smoking and that a full and public account of the balance of benefit and loss should be published. Official estimates of this balance in the USA and Canada, both of which countries have large investments in tobacco production and manufacture, show that elimination of cigarette smoking would result in greater savings than losses. There is little doubt that in this country there would be a large credit balance (see para 9. 51).

REFERENCES

1. COLE, H. (1965). 'Economic effects.' *Commonsense about Smoking.* A Penguin Special. 2nd edit. Penguin Books, Harmondsworth, pp. 40–70.

2. BERESFORD, J. C., COOPER, J., and MORRIS, J. N. (1970). In preparation.

Appendix B

Deaths Due to Cigarette Smoking

B. 1 The best available evidence on the mortality of British men according to smoking habits is provided by a study which has related deaths among a sample of 31,208 male British doctors between 1951 and 1961 to their smoking habits in 1951 [1]. To estimate the number of premature deaths associated with cigarette smoking the death rates of those doctors who were non-smokers or smokers of various numbers of cigarettes have been applied to the male United Kingdom population between the ages of 35 and 64. Knowing the distribution of smoking habits in this population, we can calculate the number of deaths that would have occurred in it in 1968, assuming that non-smoking men had the death rates of non-smoking doctors and that men smoking various quantities of cigarettes had the death rates of doctors who smoked these quantities. We can also calculate the number of deaths that would have occurred had all these men been non-smokers. The difference between these two numbers of deaths (after their correction as in para B.2) estimates the number of excess deaths associated with cigarette smoking and is referred to as the 'premature deaths associated with smoking' in 1968. The age limits of 35 and 64 have been chosen because deaths among young smokers make only a small contribution to the total, while deaths occurring after the age of 65 cause no loss of working life.

B. 2 The number of premature deaths associated with cigarette smoking is estimated as follows. In 1968 the distribution of manufactured-cigarette smoking habits (the 10 per cent of men who were pipe, cigar, and hand-rolled cigarette smokers is disregarded) in the male population aged 35–59 years was [4]:

Non-smokers	43 per cent
1–14 per day	16 per cent
15–24 per day	24 per cent
25 or more per day	17 per cent

Assuming that these percentages are applicable to each ten-year age-group from 35–64, it is found that if all men had had the death rates of doctors of the same age and smoking habits there would have been 80,358 deaths in men aged 35–64 in the United Kingdom in 1968. At the death rates of non-smoking doctors there would have been only 55,390 deaths. A correction now becomes necessary; the sample of doctors differed in many respects from the general population (para B. 4) and had lower mortality. In fact there were 99,082 deaths whereas 80,358 deaths were estimated on the basis of the doctors' death rates. To correct for the doctors' lower mortality the estimate based on non-smoking doctors' death rates must be scaled up by the ratio of the numbers of deaths actually recorded to that estimated with allowance for the smoking habits of the population, that is by $99,082/80,358 = 1.23$. The estimate of non-smokers' death rates now becomes $55,390 \times 1.23 = 68,296$. Subtraction, $99,082 - 68,296$, now shows that 30,786 deaths were associated with smoking. Rounding off gives the estimate that there were some 31,000 premature deaths associated with cigarette smoking among men aged 35–64 in the United Kingdom in 1968.

B. 3   It was necessary to scale up the direct estimates of deaths in para B. 2 because the mortality of the sample doctors was different from that in the general population. A full justification of the method would require a demonstration that, at every age and smoking level, the ratio of smokers' mortality to that of non-smokers was the same for the sample doctors and for the population, but this information is not available. Moreover, estimates based solely on the number of cigarettes smoked at any one time could be in error. The doctors' smoking habits were recorded in 1951, but after that many of them stopped smoking and their mortality rates from smoking-related diseases would therefore have been lower than those estimated for the general public on current smoking habits. There are also a number of smoking habits which increase the risk (including starting in early adolescence, smoking cigarettes to a short stub length, holding cigarettes in the mouth between puffs, and relighting old cigarettes), all of which are undoubtedly more prevalent in the general population than in doctors. Both the changes in doctors' smoking habits since 1951 and the differences between doctors and the general population would tend to cause an underestimate of the excess mortality of cigarette smokers by the method of calculation used. Although the method used can lead only to an approximation, check calculations using total death rates from the two large American studies [2, 3] give estimates of 40,000 and 35,000 for the number of premature deaths associated with cigarette smoking in 1968. The closeness of these estimates to that derived from the study of British doctors suggests that the errors are marginal.

B. 4   It is not possible to give a precise estimate of the proportion of these excess deaths among smokers which are caused by smoking. There can be little doubt that at least half of the estimated 31,000 excess deaths among male smokers aged 35–64 in the United Kingdom were due to smoking: this represents a toll of at least 15,000 deaths in men during their working life. Doll and Hill [1] suggested that a rather higher proportion, about 65 per cent of the excess deaths among smoking doctors were attributable to smoking; applying this proportion to the male population of the United Kingdom increases the estimate to about 20,000. That these estimates are not excessive can be shown by another approach. Of the 99,082 deaths in this age group 12,494 were due to lung cancer, 6,492 to chronic bronchitis and emphysema, and 31,013 to coronary heart disease. Evidence given in the report shows that cigarette smoking is the dominant factor in causing lung cancer, a very important factor in chronic bronchitis, and an important one in this age group in coronary artery disease. It would not be unreasonable to attribute to cigarette smoking 90 per cent of the deaths from lung cancer, 75 per cent of those from chronic bronchitis and 25 per cent of those from coronary artery disease. These probably conservative assumptions lead to an estimate of about 24,000 deaths from these three diseases caused by cigarette smoking among men aged 35 to 64.

B. 5 The number of deaths associated with smoking among women cannot be estimated in the same way as for men because too few women were included in the survey of British doctors [1]. But it can reasonably be assumed that at least 40 per cent of the deaths from lung cancer, 60 per cent of those from bronchitis, and 20 per cent of those from coronary heart disease in women aged 35–64 may well be due to cigarette smoking. This would indicate that some 3,500 female deaths at these ages were due to smoking in 1968 (Table 4. 1).

B. 6 At ages above 65 the number of deaths certified as due to the main smoking-related diseases is much greater than at younger ages (Table 4. 1). It would be possible to estimate the number of deaths associated with smoking in these older people by the same methods as were used at younger ages, but this could not be done with much confidence, partly because certification of the cause of death in older people, who may suffer a variety of disabilities, is less accurate than in younger people, and also because older people have a relatively short expectation of life so that its curtailment by diseases caused by smoking is of less concern than at younger ages. For these reasons no attempt has been made to estimate the number of deaths due to cigarette smoking in older people. It can only be said with confidence that many thousands of old people who are cigarette smokers die a year or two earlier than they would have done if they had not smoked cigarettes.

REFERENCES

1. DOLL, R., and HILL, A. B. (1964). 'Mortality in relation to smoking: ten years observations of British doctors.' *Brit. med. J.*, **1**, 1399 and 1460.
2. HAMMOND, E. C. (1966). 'Smoking in relation to the death rates of one million men and women.' In *Epidemiological Approaches to the Study of Cancer and Other Diseases*. Haenszel, W., Ed. Bethesda, US Public Health Service, *Nat. Cancer Inst. Monogr.*, **19**, 127–204.

3. KAHN, H. A. (1966). 'The Dorn study of smoking and mortality among US veterans: Report on eight and one half years of observation.' In *Epidemiological Approaches to the Study of Cancer and other Diseases*. Haenszel, W., Ed. Bethesda, US Public Health Service, *Nat. Cancer Inst. Monogr.*, **19**, 1–125.

4. TODD, G. F. (1969). *Statistics of Smoking in the United Kingdom*. Tobacco Research Council, Research Paper No. 1, fifth edition, p. 48.